Home Planning for Your Later Years

- **New Designs**
- **Living Options**
- **Smart Decisions**
- **How to Finance It**

For You

In the hope
that this might
stimulate some
ideas on making
gardening easier
for this
cycl group —

Bill Watch
5/97

Home Planning for Your Later Years

- **New Designs**
- **Living Options**
- **Smart Decisions**
- **How to Finance It**

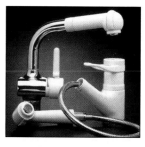

William K. Wasch
Consultant and Co-Founder
Independence Resource Center
Middletown, Connecticut

Beverly Cracom Publications

A joint venture between Beverly Foundation and Cracom Publishing

BCP ■Beverly Cracom Publications

Publisher & Editorial Director: Barbara Ellen Norwitz
Senior Editor: Donna Frassetto
Developmental Editor: Marny Johnson
Production Editor: Joy Moore
Design & Production: Mary Siener
Manufacturing: Michael Kemper

Photography: Lightworks Photography & Design, Annapolis, MD
George D. Dodson

Notice: The author and publisher of this volume have attempted to offer easy-to-use information and assessment tools that are currently accepted and used by professionals in related fields. Nevertheless, new products are continually under development, which will expand the options available to the reader and alter some of the application of concepts presented in this text. The publisher and author disclaim any liability, loss, injury, or damage incurred as a consequence, directly or indirectly, of the use and application of any of the contents of this volume.

Library of Congress Cataloging-in-Publication Data
Home Planning for Your Later Years
William K. Wasch

Includes bibliographical index

ISBN: 1-886657-07-6

1. Home planning & design 2. Home modification 3. Retirement homes & communities I. William K. Wasch

Printed in the United States of America

10 9 8 7 6 5 4 3 2 1

Foreword

Walk into any bookstore and you will see evidence of an explosion of information directed to the consumer in a "how to" format. From physical fitness to spiritual exploration, today's book market can satisfy almost any inquiry, and the number of titles focusing on the needs of those of us who are over age 50 is increasing as publishers anticipate the maturing of the baby boomers.

Curiously, however, I have never seen a readable, affordable book on how to design a retirement home. Most authors offer nifty designs for young families or empty nesters and neglect to mention architectural features that would make it easy for people to "age in place." They ignore modifications that are cheaper to incorporate into an original plan before a person needs to revamp the bathrooms, kitchen, or floor space for independent living in later years, with or without disabilities. They assume that readers will want long-term mortgages rather than reckon costs in ways that reflect the realities of most older Americans.

Home Planning for Your Later Years by William K. Wasch is valuable in filling this gap on the bookshelf. As an alumni director for a distinguished private university, Bill realized that older people were pretty savvy, with individual tastes and preferences that could not be easily merged into a single peer profile. After starting a second career in the field of aging, Bill worked with a variety of senior citizen groups, senior housing organizations, and companies in his local community and around the country. More importantly, he and his wife, Susan, built their own house. They had some lucky breaks—they found a terrific site near their hometown, and one of their children is an architect. In retrospect, Bill and Susan might have done things a bit differently, but it is precisely that practical know-how, that sense of "we've been there," that comes across on every page of this book.

Readers can trust *Home Planning for Your Later Years*. It relies on the best research available and is leavened by Bill's good common sense.

W. Andrew Achenbaum
Professor of History, University of Michigan
Acting Director, Institute of Gerontology

Credits
Hilaire Belloc verse, reprinted by permission of the Peters Fraser & Dunlop Group Ltd.

Margaret Christenson quote, from Christenson, M. *Aging in the Designed Environment.* Binghamton, NY: Hayworth Press, 1990, pp. 3-25.

Assessment in Shared Living, adapted from *Living Longer, Living Better: Adventures in Community Housing For Those in the Second Half of Life* by Jane Porcino. Copyright © 1991 by Jane Porcino. Used with permission of The Crossroad Publishing Company, New York.

Hibinfo Worksheet, adapted with permission from Barry Hibben of Hibinfo, Mill Valley, CA.

Betty Friedan quotes, reprinted with permission of Simon & Schuster from *The Fountain of Age* by Betty Friedan. Copyright © 1993 by Betty Friedan. pages 350 and 375.

Preface

Since you're reading this book, you are probably either planning your retirement or know someone who is. Either way, you deserve recognition for your pioneering spirit. The choices you make now are taking place at a time when our country is moving into a new century with a whole new definition of what it means to grow old—and a brand new set of strategies for making those later years satisfying, comfortable, healthy, and stimulating.

One of the most important decisions you make will be housing— no matter whether you decide to stay in your present home, move to another area of the country, or stay in the same community but with a different home environment. These are choices we can make now, for ourselves, ahead of time, with sound easy-to-use tools to help ensure the right decision.

So come with me on a journey through one of the biggest decisions you will make at this time of your life—where to live, what your home can and should do for you, and how to open the doors to your dreams.

I will hold my house in the high wood
Within a walk of the sea
And the men that were boys when I was a boy
Shall sit and drink with me.

The South Country
by Hilaire Belloc

Acknowledgments

This book is a tribute to the late Frank Tryon who taught me over many Saturday afternoons that all of us have the potential to function independently in our own homes in the face of severe physical limitations. Frank's long battle with arthritis was a tremendous inspiration to me and his many loyal friends. But it was not until I had a chance to work out these ideas with the help of my architect daughter, Christina, and two other talented architects, Paul Grayson and John Martin, that the main ideas in this book took form. I am most grateful for the time and energy they put into the initial "Middletown House" project that led to the writing of this book.

I also want to acknowledge the steady encouragement of my wife, Susan, and our other three children, especially Heidi, my family editor, who helped me through the various revisions. And, most of all, thanks go to my secretary, Audrey Taylor, who helped me hammer out much of this material on our word processor.

As in most writing projects, the greatest benefit personally is its way of forcing us to put into print and photo new and unfamiliar ideas. I am especially grateful to Marny Johnson, the editor of the book, for her vision and sense of organization. Special thanks also go to George Dodson, a gifted photographer, and Katie Lawyer, his able assistant. And to my publishers, Craig Cuddeback and Barbara Norwitz, thank you for recognizing the need for this type of book and having the confidence in me to publish it.

William K. Wasch
Middletown, Connecticut
December 1995

Contents

Chapter Three
Evaluating Your Resources 61

Chapter Four
Modifying Your Present Home 97

Chapter One

What to Expect

The Good News

Statistics tell us that most of us will continue to live independently for many years to come. In fact, 70% to 75% of Americans over age 65 are fully able to care for themselves. About 20% of our peers require some assistance with personal care or housekeeping and maintenance, but even these individuals are still living in their own homes. That leaves only 5% to 10% of us for whom health problems require the type of assistance offered by nursing homes and other assisted-living facilities, and most of these people receive care and support services at home, either from family and friends or from professional caregivers. The 1990 census shows that only 1% of those 65 to 74 live in nursing homes, with the number increasing to 22% after age 85 (U.S. Department of Commerce, 1993).

So we are staying home, and with formal retirement anywhere between the ages of 55 and 65, many of us will spend another 30 years in this home. What these years may offer is looking bright, indeed. Consider these findings from recent medical and scientific research:

- For many years, it was commonly believed that brain cells and mental ability diminished with age. New research, however, indicates that for healthy people—even those in their 80s—there is no deterioration in either basic mental competence or intelligence, provided they continue to be challenged intellectually.

- A National Institute of Mental Health study of healthy men found little difference in intellectual function measured by brain metabolism and blood flow between men in their 70s and 80s and men in their 20s and 30s (U.S. Department of Commerce, 1993).

- Another recent finding is that intellectual challenge—from crossword puzzles to playing a musical instrument to fixing furniture—can stimulate brain growth, and, in effect, add to the reserve capacity of the brain (thereby proving the old adage that life truly is a learning experience).

- Intellectual efforts can pay off in greater longevity, as well. In various studies, those who lived the longest demonstrated higher intellectual capacities and flexibility of mind.

So what does this have to do with decisions about your home? Two experiences shaped my own outlook and encouraged me to research and write this book.

The first was a friendship with a man in his 60s who had been crippled in his 30s by arthritis. Though wheelchair-dependent, he had created an independent lifestyle for himself in his own home. I visited my friend every week and was truly inspired by his positive outlook on life and our stimulating conversations. It was obvious that despite the risks, staying independent rather than resigning himself to the more "supportive" environment of a nursing home or assisted-living facility was the key to his happiness and self-esteem.

The second experience occurred when I visited a well-known retirement community on the West Coast. I was surprised to see attractive houses that would be great for the 50-year-old, active retiree, but would become increasingly difficult to live in as the years went by. I found that it was an up and down trip to walk through a home: narrow corridors, tight bathrooms, slippery tile

floors, and tricky slippery steps up a catwalk leading to the second floor bedrooms and bathrooms. All told, it would make everyday living for an older individual nearly impossible.

These experiences convinced me that something had to be done to make the home for our later years more responsive to our needs. Ultimately, this led to a cooperative effort with my daughter and two architects to develop a new concept home we call the "Middletown House." It is a ground level home with a lower-level accessory apartment incorporating elements of the more age-friendly design theory known as "universal" design. More information on our model home is presented in Chapter 5, but you need not build a new home to live well in your older years. With planning, we can all look forward to an older age in which we are *supported* rather than *defeated* by the structure of our home environment.

Examples From Our Peers

The Historic Farm

An 85-year-old retired professor had been living in his historic farmhouse on the outskirts of a university town for the past 40 years. He enjoyed cutting and carrying wood and gardening. His home, like so many, had the bedrooms and bath on the second floor. In recent years, he had developed failing eyesight, a hearing disability, and severe arthritis which made it difficult for him to go up and down the stairs and to stand up from a seated position.

A review of his situation by an occupational therapist offered several recommendations to make life easier for him if he chose to remain in his home. These included:

1. Improving overall illumination in work and reading areas and obtaining a low vision consultation to determine what magnifying devices might help.

2. Installing a large button telephone with an amplifier to simplify dialing and improve hearing.

3. Adding an inner wall extendible handrail which permits a user to grasp a railing on each side and makes it easier to go up and down the stairs.

4. Obtaining a chair which lifts one up from a seated position.

The Large Victorian Family Home

A couple in their late 70s with various health problems were facing increasing accessibility problems in the large home where they had raised their four children. The husband's heart problem and his wife's decreasing mobility due to arthritis seriously jeopardized their ability to be safe and fully enjoy their home.

A similar evaluation by an occupational therapist recommended:

1. Installing handrails on the open stair landing leading to the stairs to the second floor bedroom to provide more secure passage through this area.

2. Replacing the items on the top shelves of pantry closets with rarely used items.

3. Adding ramps from the garage to the main floor of the house, from the front hall to the stairs, and into the family room.

4. Relocating the washer and dryer from the basement to the kitchen pantry to eliminate walking up and down the narrow and dimly lit stairs while carrying laundry.

Updating an Already-Modified Home

A single older woman moved into a ranch-style home. Although the previous owners, an elderly couple, had already made some modifications to the house, several other changes were suggested. The fact that this home was on one floor made it easier to adapt than a multi-story home. Recommendations included:

1. Updating the alarm system to make it more user-friendly. The current unit had very small controls and was hard to see and operate.

2. Installing railings and a gradual ramp to eliminate the steep steps between the house and attached garage.

3. Improving access to the basement by installing railings and strip lighting.

4. Making a variety of kitchen and bath-room height adaptations such as replacing the toilet with a higher, easier-to-use 19-inch unit and lowering the kitchen counters to a more comfortable level for the owner.

Large Home, Tight Budget

The owners had lived in this turn-of-the-century Victorian home in the downtown area of a large city for 25 years and had made numerous modifications during this time. They were eager to stay in their house but were on a tight budget, and additional changes would need to be carefully planned. An evaluation by a builder and an occupational therapist helped them plan how they could slowly adapt their home and thus be able to stay in it for the foreseeable future.

The fundamental problem with this home, as with many others, was that two large bathrooms and all of the bedrooms were on the second floor. A careful study of the house indicated that the best long-term solution would be to convert the ground floor dining room to a bedroom and install a bathroom on the ground floor should a health crisis strike.

Also recommended were less costly changes that could be implemented over a period of time to make this home more comfortable and safe. These included:

1. Replacing the wobbly and insecure railings on both sides of the steep front steps. It was also noted that there was room to install an attractive wooden ramp directly into the house should it be necessary in the future.

2. Installing railings up to the large open landing leading to the stairs to the second floor.

3. Adding better lighting, non-slip flooring, and side railings on the dark basement stairway.

4. Exploring a variety of low-cost, but effective, alarm system options.

5. Budgeting for electronically operated overhead garage doors to replace the original, old-fashioned, hard-to-open side swinging doors.

Understanding the Variables

Health

Whether or not your retirement years have been planned in careful detail, one thing is certain: None of us can predict the future, particularly when it comes to our health. What we do know is that, as we age, there are specific changes that will affect our bodies and our lives to varying degrees. For some of us, these changes may be significant and require major adaptations; for others, aging will be a slower, subtler process of change. In either case, the ability to remain independent and lead a fulfilling life will be greatly affected by the environment we call home.

Consider these activities—opening jars, hearing the phone ring or the person we are speaking with on the phone, carrying laundry down to the basement, climbing or descending stairs, and reaching into floor-level cabinets. All of these tasks, which we take for granted when we are younger, have the potential to become more difficult as we age. Several basic modifications, however, can make most homes more age-friendly. For example, adding volume control phones, ramps for wheelchair access, grab bars in the bathroom, and easy-to-open door handles or electrical switches can produce psychological as well as physical benefits.

Perhaps you already have some conflicts with your home environment. After all, your home is static; it is not going to change for you. But you are dynamic and capable of bringing greater ease and comfort into your life by either "taming" your home or making a decision to move into new surroundings that will be more suitable to your needs.

According to the National Center for Health Statistics (1995), the ten most common chronic conditions for individuals age 65 and older, in order of frequency, are:

1. Arthritis
2. High blood pressure
3. Hearing impairment
4. Heart disease
5. Cataracts
6. Degeneration of muscles, bones, and joints
7. Chronic sinusitis
8. Diabetes
9. Visual impairment
10. Varicose veins

Although it is impossible to tell what your needs may be as you grow older, important insights can be gained from several sources.

1. Your family history: For example, did your parents or your spouse's parents have any problems in old age that might affect you or your spouse and the way you function in your home?

2. Your current level of fitness and health: For example, are you already having difficulty with activities you might once have enjoyed, such as mowing the lawn, gardening, or making minor repairs?

3. Knowledge of the normal process of change that occurs with age and the types of limitations or disabilities these changes may bring.

A brief overview of general changes that can be anticipated with aging is offered here. But, remember, there is no set time frame for these changes, and no law of science that says everyone will share the same experiences.

Functional Changes

Strength and Dexterity

Loss of strength has been ranked number one in studies asking people about their most difficult problems as they age. A close second to loss of strength is decreased manual dexterity—the loss of the ability to grip, grasp, twist, and turn items such as bottle and jar lids, door and faucet handles, and pull or push cabinet and dresser drawers.

Reach and Range of Motion

Most homes have been built to accommodate people of average height. If you are short, you may need help reaching high cabinets and shelves. If you are tall, you may have difficulty reaching into floor-level cabinets and lower shelves. Your ability to function efficiently as you grow older will depend on how easily you can stoop and stretch and kneel and raise your arms—in other words, your range of motion. Stiff joints, balance problems, or low blood pressure are just a few examples of common age-related changes that may prove limiting as you go about your daily routine.

Table 1-1	**Percent of Elders with Range of Motion Difficulties**	
	Raise Arms above Shoulders	**Stoop and Crouch**
Women (65-69)	15 %	40%
Men (65-69)	9 %	30%
Women (85+)	30 %	65%
Men (85+)	17 %	40%

(Coroni-Huntley and others, 1986)

Mobility

Our ability to move about our environment and our home depends on the condition of muscles, joints, and bones. Arthritis is the number one factor affecting the mobility of seniors, and one–half of all individuals age 65 and older have some degree of arthritis. Additionally, more than 15% of this age group suffer from some degree of muscle, bone, or joint degeneration.

For many people with these disabilities, what was once an accommodating home can become a place full of barriers, traps, and hazards. Arthritis makes it difficult to grasp and turn knobs on doors and faucets. Small buttons, snaps, and zippers on clothing can no longer be opened or closed without pain. Those suffering from arthritis find it difficult to perform such basic tasks as walking up and down stairs. In one study, more than 5% of men and nearly 10% of women between the ages 65 and 69, and almost 20% of men and 33% of women age 85 and older could not climb the stairs in their own homes (Coroni-Huntley and others, 1986). Such disability makes using second floor bedrooms and bathrooms impossible. If the upper body is affected by arthritis, reaching under a kitchen cabinet or taking something off an upper shelf can be difficult and painful.

The loss of muscle mass and strength, along with bone deterioration can make such normal activities as bathing, grooming, and dressing a daily challenge. Rising from a deep-seated position or using the toilet also becomes difficult. These disabilities also increase the risk of falling—one of the most common and serious types of accidents suffered by older people.

If interior doorways and corridors are narrow, it can be awkward for individuals to maneuver with a wheelchair, walker, or cane. Foregoing the stability offered by a cane or walker in order to enter the bathroom or reach an electrical outlet close to the floor can, again, increase the risk of a fall.

Balance and Coordination

Receptor nerves located throughout the joints, tendons, and muscles, as well as in the inner ear, provide us with our sense of balance. This ability is what enables us to sense the weight of objects, how and where we are moving, and how the body is positioned. With gradual loss of this ability older people are increasingly unsteady and have increased risk of falls. In fact, many falls and injuries occur in the dark when visual clues are not available to aid our balance.

Cognition

Aging also affects reaction time and the number of external stimuli we can process at one time. Our ability to think does not change, but our ability to sort out competing, or multiple, inputs and to perceive the stimuli in our environment does. For example, one product which would help offset this factor is an electric stove control which becomes brighter and redder as the temperature is turned up.

The Senses

Proper lighting makes it possible to continue hobbies.

Sight. As we age, our eyes adjust to dark more slowly. At the age of 30, the eyes need just 2 to 3 minutes to adjust to the dark; by the age of 80, however, they need 10 minutes. In the course of aging, the lens of the eye yellows, which decreases depth perception and increases sensitivity to glare. Judging the level and depth of stairs, the edges of furniture, or where one wall meets another can become difficult. One solution suggested in the work of Margaret Christenson, an occupational therapist whose research has emphasized aging and the home environment, is to use contrasting colors to alleviate depth perception problems and make it easier to recognize objects in the home.

By the age of 50, most people have begun noticing changes in the ability to see. As the lens of the eye loses elasticity, a person may have difficulty focusing on the details of objects either up close or at varied distances. As the lens becomes less transparent and thickens, a person requires more light to see properly. In fact, an 80-year-old person requires three times as much light as a 20-year-old individual. Another obstacle for older people is the rapid flicker of fluorescent lights, which can cause severe eye strain. As the need for more light increases, so does one's sensitivity to glare—for example, from sunlight reflected off polished floors or stainless steel appliances.

In addition to improving the lighting conditions in your home, replacing objects and repainting walls from pastels to more vibrant colors is also recommended. Reds and yellows, rather than blue, beige, yellow or pink will improve the contrast between floors, walls, doors, and so forth.

The inclusion of prominent features or landmarks of different colors in the design of a home's interior can also make it easier for older persons to orient themselves to location. By making your environment structured, predictable, and visually rich, as well as brighter and with more contrast you will reduce your tendency to "grope" for a secure footing or balance and will feel more secure as you move about your home.

Hearing. Hearing provides constant surveillance, permitting us to hear something before we see it. This early warning system even continues to function as we sleep. However, more than 30% of people age 65 and older have lost some hearing ability. Such losses can be caused by a variety of conditions other than aging, including injury, heredity, and long-term exposure to loud noise.

Age-related hearing impairment may take various forms. Most often, sounds appear softer than they actually are. Individuals with this type of problem can usually raise the volume of their television or radio to compensate.

Presbycusis is another common problem that can affect older people. This condition occurs when the nerve endings and auditory hair cells in the inner ear are damaged, resulting in a decline in sound clarity. Individuals with presbycusis often complain that voices sound garbled. Another common form of hearing loss affects the ability to hear high tones particularly when speaking on the telephone or using other electronic devices. This can usually be improved by adjusting sound frequencies on these types of equipment.

Still another type of hearing impairment is difficulty in locating and identifying higher-frequency sounds. For a person with this problem, the ability to hear smoke and fire alarms can be limited. This can be remedied by installing safety and security systems that incorporate visual cues, such as flashing lights.

Lack of concentration and insecurity can result from hearing impairments that affect the ability to distinguish specific sounds from background noise. Listening to the radio can become almost impossible when noises from other rooms and outside the house blend together to create a blanket of unrecognizable sounds.

Although hearing aids have improved considerably in recent years, the operation of smaller-sized hearing aids may require fine hand and finger control that is difficult for the older person with reduced strength and dexterity.

Smell. The sense of smell also declines with age. A 65-year-old person has about 10% of the capacity that a 15-year-old has to discriminate among odors. Such reduced sensory function poses a serious danger for seniors, who have a seven-fold higher mortality rate in residential fires than younger individuals. A reduced sense of smell also makes it difficult to detect airborne pollution and toxins that could impair safety in the home.

Another problem related to the reduced sense of smell is a loss of appetite. Foods such as bacon or fresh-baked desserts that are enticing by their aroma may become less appealing.

Taste. We possess the ability to taste four components: sweet, salt, bitter, and sour. As we grow older our taste buds are considerably diminished. An 80-year-old adult has only about one–third as many taste buds as a 30-year-old. Research suggests that older men are more likely to want more salt on their foods than older women (Christensen, 1990). An increase in the use of condiments, particularly sugar and salt, is favored by seniors, but unfortunately these are not the healthiest of choices. Various herbs and spices can be substituted for salt and provide food with more taste appeal. Kitchen and dining facilities should therefore be designed for easy access to condiments.

Touch. As we age, our skin sensitivity as well as our perception of temperature diminishes. This can be dangerous, because with the loss of these functions, the risk of thermal injuries such as scalding and freezing increases.

As other senses are impaired, older persons may compensate by relying more on their sense of touch. Home modifications that increase tactile input can be helpful. For example, installing carpeting over a hard wood floor can reduce glare, add warmth to the room, and improve mobility. Distinctive additions to any surface, such as brick, vinyl or wood, can become guides for the visually impaired person. Touch can also be a source of comfort, for example, the familiar texture of a favorite chair.

User-Friendly Ideas and Designs

Over the past several years, architects, interior designers, and urban planners have become more sensitive to the needs of the disabled when designing buildings and homes. Additionally, state and federal regulations now require that businesses, government buildings, and public transportation be made accessible for the handicapped. These changes have proven equally beneficial to older people who may be experiencing a variety of functional changes limiting their mobility.

The field of industrial engineering has provided some major breakthroughs in design concepts that are considered user-friendly, and specifically tailored to improve the quality of life for all individuals. These design concepts can be grouped into two specific types:

• **Universal design**—Also referred to as "life cycle" or "life span" design, universal design is sensitive to all users, of all ages, taking into consideration periods of temporary, permanent, or progressive disability.

• **Human factors design**—Also referred to as "user-based" design, human factors design addresses human characteristics and behaviors, specifically the way people use objects and materials at home and at work.

The physical changes encountered as we age ultimately involve many complex social, political, design, and medical issues, and solutions draw upon the resources of several disciplines. Ideally, design team members should include architects, engineers, interior designers, urban planners, environmental psychologists, gerontologists, physical and occupational therapists, builders, and contractors who work together to interpret the needs of the "user"—who is undoubtedly the most important member of this multidisciplinary team. Even in the best-case scenarios, however, it is doubtful any one person will have the resources to hire all of these individuals to assist in the design or redesign of a home.

It is important, then, to ensure that whoever you do enlist to assist you has the proper credentials necessary for the task at hand. When hiring professional help to assist you in your endeavors, it is imperative that they understand the major barriers to comfort, safety, and mobility that will be involved. Such barriers include those that are defined as physical, functional, and perceptual.

Barriers to Comfort, Safety, and Mobility

Narrow doors and hallways can make maneuvering with a wheelchair or walker difficult.

Physical barriers are described as anything that impinges on the actual performance of a task. These are usually most easily remedied with the help of an architect, and are, therefore, often referred to as structural or architectural barriers, as well. Examples of interior physical barriers include:

- Doors and hallways too narrow for the passage of a wheelchair or other ambulatory-assistive device

- Toilet seats that are too high or low

- Stairs with risers that are too high and treads that are too shallow

- Steps or uneven surfaces

- Paper towel or other paper dispensers that are inconvenient to reach

- Poor lighting or glare on reflective surfaces

Examples of external physical barriers include:

- Narrow doorways or difficult-to-manipulate door handles and locks
- Stairs

- Curbs

- Sidewalks that are sloped too steeply

- Uneven surfaces

Functional barriers are objects or tools that may be difficult to use by the person who is experiencing any type of physical limitation. Examples of functional barriers include:

- Can openers requiring the use of both hands or designed only for right-hand use

- Packaging, especially of medications or drugs, that is difficult to open and places vital information in very small print

- Any type of printed instruction that is difficult to follow or keep in correct order, especially for medications, food preparation, or use of tools and appliances

- Containers for storage that are too difficult to open or close

A steep slope or stairway leading to an entrance can provide a barrier.

- Bathtubs that are slippery and hard to access

Sensory barriers are conditions that impair the ability to see, hear, and taste or to discriminate by touch and smell. These include:

- Poor lighting in dark areas such as in basement stairways, glare from light or reflective surfaces, and low levels of natural light in outdoor areas, such as patios

- External noise from traffic and other outside sources; internal or "ambient" noise such as voices as well as lack of proper sound barriers between floors

- Uncontrolled water heater thermostats, unmonitored natural gas emissions, auditory-only fire and smoke alarms, stovetop heating elements that do not give visible clues to temperature

Chemical barriers are indoor pollutants that are often not detectable without specialized testing devices. Energy-efficient structures may recycle gases from building materials and furnishings, creating a "sick house" syndrome. If left unchecked, they may impair the health of the individual. Examples of chemical barriers are:

- Carbon monoxide from unventilated heating systems

- Asbestos insulation

- Radon gas

An architect can design changes to improve access to your home.

Your Personal Forecast

Although it is best to work with an occupational therapist for a complete assessment designed for an individual's range of abilities, the following three audits, which focus on home and personal needs, attitude, and ability to carry out activities, are a good place to start. They are particularly helpful for initial planning when a family is faced with the "empty nest" syndrome or with assisting a parent in his or her own home who must cope with a recent disability.

The Personal Preferences and Needs Assessment that follows is geared to a family in their 50s who are beginning to think about housing options for their later years. Next is the Detailed Personal Abilities Assessment, which is geared to an older, frailer group. Finally, the Activities of Daily Living Assessment assesses the ability to carry out everyday activities. These audits illustrate the types of questions those of all ages should consider as they assess their personal situation and begin to plan for future housing needs.

Personal Preferences and Needs Assessment

This audit form will help a family in their 50s assess their future housing needs.

1. *How long have you been in your home?* _____ *Years*

2. *Have you done any major remodeling?* _____ *Yes* _____ *No*

   If so, what major project(s) did you complete and when?

3. *Is it necessary/desirable to continue to live in your present community?*

   _____ *Yes* _____ *No*

   If so, why would you choose to do so?

   _____ We want to live near our children who live within 50 miles.

   _____ A high priority for us is seeing our nearby grandchildren every week.

   _____ We must stay in this community to care for an elderly parent.

   _____ We have made lifelong friends in this community, and our social life revolves around our relationship with them.

   _____ When I retire, I plan to continue to work part-time, and it is important for me to remain in this area because of my potential business contacts here.

4. *Do you wish to move to another area of the country?*

   _____ *Yes* _____ *No*

   If so, why would you choose to do so?

   _____ We want to move closer to my elderly parents.

   _____ We want to live near our children who live within 50 miles.

   _____ For us a high priority is seeing our grandchildren as often as possible, and this move would bring us within 50 miles of them.

   _____ When I retire, moving to this area of the country will give me many more opportunities to start a new business doing work in which I am interested.

   _____ The climate is more favorable for relief of physical symptoms (for example, symptoms caused by arthritis).

5.   *Do you have any plans to move out of this home in the foreseeable future?*

_____ Yes _____ No

If so, what other housing alternatives are you considering?

_____ Move to a retirement area of country, for example, Florida, North Carolina?

_____ Move to a rental retirement community, assisted-living facility, continuing care retirement community (CCRC)?

_____ Move to an apartment or a single family house nearer children?

_____ Other possibilities? If so, please describe them.

_____

6.   *Are health problems preventing you from doing what you want to do?*

_____ Yes _____ No

If so, what are general areas of concern that affect your housing needs?

_____ Arthritis

_____ Visual and/or hearing difficulties

_____ Other concerns such as heart, emphysema, and so forth.

7.   *Do you have a disability that makes it difficult for you to do daily activities?*

_____ Yes _____ No

If so, describe it briefly.

_____

What areas of your home should be made more accessible?

_____ *Kitchen*

_____ *Bedroom*

_____ *Bathroom*

_____ *Halls and stairs*

_____ *Yard and/or other area (describe)*

_____

8.   *What house and yard activities do you enjoy doing but cannot do now?*

_____ Cleaning

_____ Gardening

_____ Reading

_____ Telephoning

_____ Watching television or VCR; listening to radio or stereo

_____ Other (describe)

_____

9.   *Do you enjoy cooking and using your kitchen?*

_____ Yes _____ No

10.   *Are your bathing and showering facilities adequate?*

_____ Yes _____ No

If inadequate, please note specific needs.

_____ Are bath, shower, toilet, and vanity accessible?

_____ Could you benefit from easier entry, better lighting, or other changes?

11.   *Do you have difficulty climbing stairs?*

_____ Yes, need some help

_____ Yes, unable

_____ No

Detailed Personal Abilities Assessment

This audit form is designed for individuals who are beginning to experience physical and/or sensory limitations. This form should help you or the person you are assisting develop an awareness of present and possible future physical and sensory limitations, and how they may influence the ability to perform various tasks in and around the house. After completing this form, you will be able to determine what needs should be addressed now, and in the future.

Special Note: *If you are completing this form for someone else, be sure that you are provided with adequate input for each question. Carefully assess all areas described in this form. If you are completing this form for yourself, be honest with yourself about your present conditions and future needs.*

1.   *I live with:*

_____ Spouse

_____ Children

_____ Friend or relative

_____ Alone

_____ Other (explain)

_____

2.   *The people who live with me, and their ages are:*

_____

3.   *When I need help around the house (cleaning, moving things, cooking, etc.) I can count on assistance from:*

_____

4.   *I get around the house by:*

_____ Walking

_____ Walking with a cane, crutches, or walking aid

_____ Using a wheelchair

_____ Using a power scooter

_____ Other (explain)

_____

5.   *I have problems with:*

_____ Arthritis	_____ Orthopedic impairments
_____ Strength	_____ Coordination
_____ Reaching and stretching	_____ Balance
_____ Use of hands	_____ Disorientation
_____ Dressing and undressing	_____ Breathing
_____ High blood pressure	_____ Vision
_____ Heart disease	_____ Cataracts
_____ Diabetes	_____ Hearing

6.   *I have problems with my vision, specifically:*

_____ Sharpness of vision	_____ Double vision
_____ Depth perception	_____ Changes in light intensity
_____ Distinguishing colors	

7. *I have problems with my hearing, specifically:*

_____ Difficulty in hearing well in the presence of loud sounds

_____ Interference from background noise

_____ Recognizing where sound is coming from

_____ Understanding what people are saying

_____ Needing to turn the volume on my television and radio higher

8. *I have difficulty with:*

_____ Grasping small objects (doorknobs, buttons, control knobs, utensils)

_____ Lifting objects

_____ Maintaining a steady grasp

_____ Reaching forward

_____ Reaching high objects

_____ Bending or stooping down for items on the floor or under counters

9. *I enjoy, but have difficulty with: Explain.*

_____ Cleaning

_____

_____ Cooking

_____

_____ Reading

_____

_____ Talking on telephone

_____

_____ Listening to TV and radio

_____

_____ Gardening

_____

_____ Outdoor maintenance

_____

10.   *I am concerned about:*

_____ Being helpless if something happened at home and no one knew

_____ Moving around the house without slipping or falling

_____ Feeling safe while alone in my home

Activities of Daily Living Assessment

Listed below are typical activities and tasks involved in independent living. Carefully review each item listed under the six categories and select the appropriate response.

Level of importance: 1 = Very important

2 = Important

3 = Not important

Level of ability: A = I can now do this easily by myself.

B = I can do this now by myself with some difficulty (explain).

C = With some modification now, I could do this by myself (explain).

D = The physical environment may need to be modified in the future so that I may continue doing this activity or task (explain).

After completing this form, you will be able to determine what activities and tasks are being met by obstacles, and what areas of the home could be adapted or modified to make your environment safer, more convenient, and comfortable.

Activity/Task	Level of Importance	Level of Ability	Please Explain
Vision			
Seeing in entryway	_____	_____	_____
Locating outside door locks	_____	_____	_____
Seeing in hallways	_____	_____	_____

Activity/Task	Level of Importance	Level of Ability	Please Explain
Going up and down stairs	_____	_____	_____
Using basement stairs	_____	_____	_____
Using attic stairs	_____	_____	_____
Moving about in basement	_____	_____	_____
Moving about in attic	_____	_____	_____
Seeing in bedroom	_____	_____	_____
Seeing in kitchen	_____	_____	_____
Seeing in bathroom	_____	_____	_____
Locating light switches	_____	_____	_____
Moving about at night	_____	_____	_____
Reading information on appliances	_____	_____	_____
Using telephones	_____	_____	_____

Hearing

Activity/Task	Level of Importance	Level of Ability	Please Explain
Hearing alarm clock	_____	_____	_____
Listening to TV or stereo	_____	_____	_____
Hearing doorbell	_____	_____	_____
Hearing someone knocking	_____	_____	_____
Hearing telephone ring	_____	_____	_____
Hearing smoke alarm	_____	_____	_____

Mobility and Accessibility

Activity/Task	Level of Importance	Level of Ability	Please Explain
Turning lights on and off	_____	_____	_____
Reaching and reading thermostats	_____	_____	_____

Activity/Task	Level of Importance	Level of Ability	Please Explain
Reaching electrical outlets	_____	_____	_____
Using door locks	_____	_____	_____
Retrieving mail	_____	_____	_____
Using knobs and controls on appliances	_____	_____	_____
Using knobs and controls on light fixtures and cabinets	_____	_____	_____
Walking between and around furniture without bumping	_____	_____	_____
Sitting down and getting up from seated position	_____	_____	_____
Going up and down stairs	_____	_____	_____
Moving through hallways	_____	_____	_____
Moving through doorways	_____	_____	_____
Making bed	_____	_____	_____
Opening and closing windows	_____	_____	_____
Reaching clothes in closet	_____	_____	_____
Dressing and undressing	_____	_____	_____
Reaching stored items	_____	_____	_____

Comprehension and Safety

Activity/Task	Level of Importance	Level of Ability	Please Explain
Moving about in dimly lit areas of house	_____	_____	_____
Remembering important phone numbers and addresses	_____	_____	_____
Using fire extinguishers	_____	_____	_____

Activity/Task	Level of Importance	Level of Ability	Please Explain
Calling for help in emergencies	_____	_____	_____
Adjusting water temperatures for bath or shower	_____	_____	_____
Maintaining proper indoor temperatures	_____	_____	_____
Using hot appliances	_____	_____	_____
Carrying groceries and packages	_____	_____	_____
Kitchen			
Reaching items in refrigerator and freezer	_____	_____	_____
Reaching items in kitchen cabinets	_____	_____	_____
Cleaning kitchen floor	_____	_____	_____
Preparing meals	_____	_____	_____
Eating	_____	_____	_____
Filling pot with water	_____	_____	_____
Reaching appliance controls	_____	_____	_____
Using appliance controls	_____	_____	_____
Moving around in kitchen	_____	_____	_____
Lifting heavy objects	_____	_____	_____
Washing dishes in sink	_____	_____	_____
Putting food in and removing from oven	_____	_____	_____
Reaching and using microwave	_____	_____	_____

Activity/Task	Level of Importance	Level of Ability	Please Explain
Seeing food cook on back burners of stove	_____	_____	_____
Reaching cookware on back burners of stove	_____	_____	_____
Reading labels on the appliances	_____	_____	_____
Opening and closing cabinet doors and drawers	_____	_____	_____
Using washer and dryer	_____	_____	_____
Retrieving items from washing machine	_____	_____	_____

References

Christensen, Margaret. *Aging in the Designed Environment.* Binghamton, N.Y.: The Haworth Press, 1990, pp. 3-25

Coroni-Huntley J., D.B. Breck, A.M. Ostfield, J.D. Taylor, and R.B. Wallace. *Established Populations for Epidemiologic Studies of the Elderly.* N.I.H. Publication No. 86-2443. Washington, D.C.: National Institute on Aging, 1986.

National Center for Health Statistics. *Trends in the Health of Older Americans: United States, 1994.* Series 3, No. 30. U.S. Department of Health and Human Services, April 1995, pp. 67-130.

U.S. Department of Commerce. *Profiles of America's Elderly.* No. 4. Washington, D.C.: Economics and Statistics Administration, November 1993.

Suggested Readings

Butler, Robert N. *Why Survive? Being Old in America.* New York: Harper & Row, 1975.

Cohen, Evelyn, and Jon Pynoos. *The Perfect Fit: Creative Ideas for a Safe and Livable Home.* Washington, D.C.: AARP Consumer Affairs Section, 1992.

Culler, Kathleen, Janet Lisak, and Marlene Morgan. *The "Safe Home" Checkout Manual.* Chicago: Geriatric Environments for Living and Learning, 1991.

Dychtwald, Ken, and Joe Flower. *Age Wave.* Los Angeles: Jeremy P. Tarcher, 1989.

Pauson, Cindy, Rannell Dahl, and William Wasch. Eliminating Architectural Barriers: A Multidisciplinary Approach. *Topics in Geriatric Rehabilitation*, vol. 9, no. 2, edited by Carole B. Lewis. Frederick, Md.: Aspen Publications, 1993.

Chapter Two

Evaluating Your Options

The Big Decision

Now that you have some ideas about what to expect as you grow older, you can begin to take steps toward a well-informed decision about your future living situation. The options are numerous:

- Stay home and modify your present home to better suit your needs

- Stay in the same community but move to a different setting

- Build a new custom-designed home

- Move to another region of the country where you can choose among several housing options

Many factors will be a part of this big decision. It is important to investigate all of these factors and weigh the pros and cons of each of them before charting a course of action. This chapter will help you identify the many specific avenues that are available to you.

Location, Location, Location

The personal assessments discussed in Chapter 1 can be helpful in determining which factors are most important to you. For some people, remaining near family and friends or living in a warm climate are essential for enjoying life. For other people, these considerations may be secondary to other priorities. When making a decision to remain in an area because friends or family are nearby, be sure to consider their future plans. In today's transient society one can no longer count on anyone remaining in the same place. Another important point to consider is the status of your neighborhood. For example, have there been significant changes in property values, demographics, overall maintenance, or the number of houses for sale in recent years? Do these factors have other advantages such as the likelihood that family and friends will also remain in the area and that real estate values will improve? Additional considerations include:

- Is the location ideal for you now and will this remain so in the future?

- Is it close to your church or synagogue?

- Are shopping facilities nearby?

- Are you involved in community groups you enjoy?

- Are property taxes affordable and likely to stay that way?

- Do you enjoy the changing seasons, or are you having increasing difficulty with extreme cold or hot weather?

How Does Your Home Measure Up?

By reviewing the following list of adaptations that can make your home more responsive to the aging process, you will begin to evaluate your home against a set of accessibility guidelines. These potential design solutions are by no means complete, but

This garage has a ramp to the house interior.

Levered handles accommodate those with decreased manual dexterity.

they do eliminate many of the basic structural, functional, and sensory barriers discussed in Chapter 1 that can impinge on your ability to live comfortably in your home. This section will also serve as a general background to the more detailed discussions in the later chapters on modifying your present home or building a completely accessible new home.

Garage and Home Entry

- Automatic garage door opener.

- A ramp with no more than a 1 inch rise for every 12 inches in length to provide at least one accessible entrance to the house, preferably from the garage if it is attached. Another option is to build an earth berm or bridge to move from the lower to the higher level entrance.

- A railing on the ramp and a shelf nearby where groceries can be placed before being brought into the house.

- Levered handles with a single lock or electronic key security system on all exterior doors.

- Swinging house-entry doors wide enough for wheelchair or walker access. A total 36-inch clear width should be allowed for at least one of the doors, particularly the one for which a ramp has been constructed.

Well-lit stairs decrease the risk of falls.

Lighting

- Fixtures with increased wattage and/or task-lighting units adjacent to high-use locations.

- Standard light switches replaced with light switches that can be seen in the dark. Rocker- or touch-control switches are other options.

- Switches and thermostats placed no higher than 48 inches above the floor and electrical outlets at least 27 inches above the floor.

- Dimmer switches to increase the intensity of lighting. Fluorescent or other tube-type lights installed along basement, attic, or other dark stairs. All stairwells and hallways should be as brightly lit as possible.

- Blinds or shades to control glare from outdoor light.

Floors

- Slip-resistant and well-lighted floors.

- Insulating materials to reduce sound transfer between floors.

- Rug corners and edges and area rugs that have been secured so they do not slide. Skid-proof pads are available and are recommended.

- Non-glare and low-gloss finishes.

- Heavy-weight, high-density, short-pile, level carpets to permit easier movement especially for wheelchair or walker users.

Stairs

- Handrails at the proper height on both sides of the stairway that extend to the bottom step so a person with a visual difficulty can easily move to the bottom.

- Non-slip treads with consistent risers and stair treads. A 7-inch riser and an 11-inch tread are recommended. If necessary, mark the edge of each tread with a color-contrast strip.

- A chair lift or extendible handrail, or the feasibility of installing these devices in the future, if mobility is severely restricted. Allow for proper space to install these features.

Hallways and Walls

- Handrails in the hallways for easy access from room to room.

- Textured wallpaper or matte paint finishes to reduce glare.

- Electrical outlets placed higher than standard, ideally 27 inches from the floor, in various convenient locations.

One-Story Living and Caregiver Housing Considerations

- Both a bathroom and a bedroom that are on the ground floor. Consider converting a den or dining room into a bedroom and remodeling or adding a bathroom with wheelchair accessibility.

- Consider the possibility of a separate bedroom and bath for a future caregiver, should you someday require live-in assistance.

Kitchen

- Kitchen that can be converted for wheelchair accessibility. All cabinets should include lazy Susans in corners, easy gliding hardware, and "C" or "D" shaped handles; cabinet fronts should be able to be easily removed especially below counters and sinks; and shelving and counters should be adjustable.

Handrails on both walls aid mobility.

Stoves with front controls enable the wheel-chair-bound individual to prepare meals.

Courtesy Whirlpool Home Appliance, Benton Harbor, Michigan

Grab bars and tub or shower seats increase bathing safety.
Courtesy Hewi, Inc., Lancaster, Pennsylvania

Leaving the sink open underneath provides wheelchair access.

- Stoves with controls in front; double-sided sinks with temperature-controlled, levered faucet handles and spray attachments; garbage disposal; trash compactor; side-by-side self-defrosting refrigerator; easy-to-use microwave oven.

Bathrooms

It is important to recognize that bathrooms are usually too small. Considerable thought and planning will be required to modify the space and improve accessibility and safety. The following features can help in your planning.

- Completely accessible bathroom with reinforced walls and blocking between 32 and 54 inches from the floor to enable future installation of anchored grab bars, for both bath and shower. A roll-in or walk-in shower with a seat and a thermostatically controlled hot water unit (to prevent scalding) with a flexible shower hose and hand-held shower head are also recommended. Consider touchless sink faucets with heat sensor contacts.

- Sink with levered handles that is low enough for use from a wheelchair.

- Toilets that are higher than average, approximately 19 inches from the floor, or contain a height-adjusting feature, with backing for the installation of grab bars.

- A pocket door which can be helpful in making the bathroom more accessible for a wheelchair.

- Non-skid flooring. Tiles are much too slippery and can be very dangerous.

Closets and Storage

- Closets that are easy to open and provide easy access to items inside. Sufficient lighting should be provided.

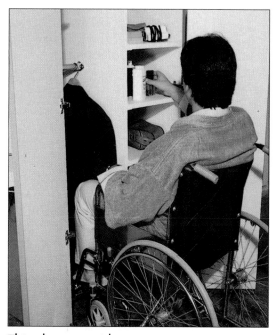

This closet provides easy access.
Courtesy BPS Architectural Products, Houston, Texas

General

- Level thresholds between rooms and areas.

- Central control and automation for appliances and security systems.

Level thresholds and pocket doors make room-to-room mobility possible for an individual using a walker or wheelchair.

Non-Traditional Options

Most of us are familiar with some of the alternative housing arrangements that have been developed in recent years. These include retirement communities and apartment complexes with various minimum age requirements. Other important concepts are also continuously being developed and tested to address the broad range of interests and needs of the growing population of older adults in the United States. More than one alternative may appeal to you as a solution for specific needs at different ages. Initially, you may want to modify your present home; but in the future, selling your home or sharing it with another individual may better suit your needs. When beginning to plan for your future housing needs, it is wise to consider all of your options.

Cohousing

Cohousing is a movement that began in Scandinavia, but is gaining popularity in the United States. Two architects, Katherine McCamant and her husband, Charles Durret, published the definitive book on the program in 1988. The book, *Cohousing: A Contemporary Approach to Housing Ourselves,* describes a group of people who wish to share some common spaces but maintain private living and sleeping areas. They purchase land together, then build their own separate homes and a large community building.

Illustrative of the program for older families is the "Cheesecake" project located about 100 miles north of San Francisco in California's Mendocino County. The project has 11 partners, all in their 50s and 60s, and consists of four married couples and three women. With the help of a landscape architect, the group found a site in a grove of redwoods and then hired another architect who took them through the planning and building process. The end result was two main buildings with seven separate living apartments and considerable common space for a large communal kitchen, a library, and a laundry and sewing area. A third structure is a large shed used for hobbies. All three units are connected by covered walkways. The architect developed contingency plans for adding ramps and an elevator for any future aging needs of the residents, and all doors are wide enough for wheelchairs. Guidelines have been written and agreed upon by the group regarding the use of the common spaces and the installation of satellite dishes, as well as the sharing of facsimile machines and computers. The group refers to their project as a "commune for growing old, actively."

Another example of cohousing is a group of 25 children and 45 adults of all ages who have established a community on Bainbridge Island, a 30-minute ferry ride from Seattle. With the assistance of architect Edward Weinstein, they have built a group of attached homes with one- and two-bedroom apartments clustered in three neighborhoods. A 6,000-square-foot common house containing the community kitchen, dining and meeting rooms, day-care center, teen room, recreation center, and laundry room serve the needs of all residents.

Unlike lifecare communities with on-site healthcare facilities, cohousing is based on democratic principles and the members' desires for a more social home environment, usually in an intergenerational setting. The cohousing situations are actually patterned after a Danish concept, called the Bofaellesskab community, in which people of all ages lived and neighbors knew and helped one another.

Advantages

- Lower cost per resident
- Mutual support, especially between age groups
- Exchange of heavy yard work for child care
- Greater social interaction and security

Disadvantages

- Inflexibility of zoning codes in many communities prohibiting a cohousing building design
- Difficulty of getting a large group of people to agree on general guidelines for the community such as meal arrangements and cooking
- Transference of ownership in the future
- Some compromise of individuality in order to reach a consensus among all the residents

Shared Housing

Between 1981 and 1987, the number of home-matching non-profit organizations in the United States rose from 40 to 400, and placed an estimated 15,000 people in small shared housing arrangements.

Shared housing is an alternative in which space is offered to a non-relative in a single family home or a group of people rent or purchase a home together. There is an agreed-upon arrangement clarifying how living space, home life, household expenses, maintenance responsibilities, chores, and sometimes social life are shared. A one-to-one sharing situation brings together two unrelated people to live in one of their apartments or homes. Small-group living involves three or more unrelated people in a similar set-up.

Combining privacy and companionship in a friendly, supportive environment is economical, practical, and socially gratifying. In addition to sharing expenses and responsibilities, housemates and roommates often consider their relationship a new type of family. Additionally, such sharing increases property ownership or rental options that simply would not be available on one income. Success in such a living arrangement requires one basic rule: mutual respect among all individuals sharing the environment.

Perhaps the most popular example of the shared housing concept was featured in the television show, "The Golden Girls," which focused on the problems and successes of four older women sharing a home. Between 1981 and 1987, the number of home-matching non-profit organizations in the United States rose from 40 to 400, and placed an estimated 15,000 people in small shared housing arrangements. The late Maggie Kuhn, founder of the Gray Panthers, lived in a small-group housing arrangement for 25 years.

The Molly Hare Cooperative in Durham, North Carolina, is an excellent example of a real-life, working shared housing environment. The founder, Elizabeth Freeman, a long-time advocate of cooperative living, purchased a small apartment house near Duke University. Within walking distance of shops and services, the building contains six apartments occupied by six women. Each owns a modern, energy-efficient unit in the building, as well as membership in the cooperative, which costs approximately $8,000. Should a member decide to leave, this fee is refundable; however, while one remains a member it provides lifelong occupancy rights and a tax deduction. Each member of the Molly Hare Cooperative must also pay a monthly rent ranging from $300 to $500, depending on the size of the apartment. The six women share meals in each others' apartments, go out at night to movies, concerts, and special events, work together in the yard, take classes together, help each other in times of illness, and provide transportation for one another as needed. All of the members consider their arrangement to be a mutually beneficial relationship for all.

Although there are many variations in living arrangements, economics is usually the factor that determines how much space or property one will be able to afford. Ideally, a separate apartment with common meeting and recreation areas seems to be the current preference among those in shared housing environments. Yet, for a lower cost, a person might just have a private bedroom space and share all other rooms in the house.

Because of the growth of home sharing and the large increase in non-profit programs that facilitate home sharing, assistance in making these arrangements is becoming more available nationwide. Perhaps the best resource for information on shared housing is the National Shared Housing Resource Center, 321 East 25th Street, Baltimore, MD 21218 (410/235-4454).

Advantages

- Lower living costs
- Benefits of an extended "family"
- Shared rent or mortgage payments, as well as household chores
- Health benefits from assistance with minor crises and illnesses
- Increased sense of security, safety, companionship, and independence

Disadvantages

- Compatibility—If the matching process is not handled carefully, serious problems can arise. Most good matching programs screen for financial and personality considerations. Issues such as pets, children, smoking, alcohol use, religious beliefs, as well as other social issues must be considered carefully.
- Zoning laws—Many areas of the country will not allow unrelated people to live together in a single family house, although variances are beginning to be awarded for people in specific circumstances.
- Transferring ownership in the future may be difficult.
- Some compromise of individuality occurs in order to reach a consensus among all residents.

Assessment in Shared Housing

The following questions were developed by Jane Porcino in her book *Living Longer and Better* (1991). These questions may prove helpful in determining whether a shared housing arrangement is a viable option for an individual considering this possibility.

1. *Would it be better for me to share my home or to become a home sharer in another house?*

    Most people report that it is often difficult to move into a home that is already established. The best case scenario may be for those who agree to share space to purchase or rent a new dwelling that can be established together.

2. *How much rent will I be able to pay?* Chapter 3 offers several assessment guidelines and checklists.

3. *How many people will I feel comfortable living with?*

    Very small groups (i.e., two to five people) may be vulnerable to strong personalities or relationships that are too intense. In addition, if one of the members suffers a serious illness or leaves the group, the vacancy can create a devastating financial hardship for the remaining members. Groups of six to fifteen people seem to be large enough for people to choose their friends and allow for a larger pool from which to draw housing costs, and divide chores and responsibilities more equally.

4. *Should I look for an "extended family," a friendly but separate relationship within my new home, or a tenant/landlord relationship?*

5. *How will I find like-minded people with compatible needs?*

    Each person investigating small group-living possibilities should question whether they want to live with someone their own age, or younger or older; with only members of their own gender, or with both women and men; with only single people or couples; or with those still working or solely with retirees. Other considerations include your basic lifestyle requirement. Are you generally neat or can you tolerate clutter? Does noise disturb you? How do you feel about pets, overnight guests, or any other issues you may have taken for granted when living alone or with your spouse? Whenever possible, a trial living arrangement of a week or more is recommended.

6. *Where would I like to live?*

    Location is extremely important. Accessibility to stores, transportation, health services, and cultural, educational, and entertainment events should all be considered. As discussed earlier in this chapter, whether or not you wish to remain near family members or friends is also an important consideration.

7. *Will I still be driving my own car?*

    In many communities located in suburban or rural areas, owning a car or being able to share rides with another member of the group is imperative.

8. *How much private space do I require?*

   A room of one's own is essential for solitude, a base of operations, and a retreat from the stimulation, expectations, and natural tensions of group living. You should also consider whether you need a private bathroom, a living area space to entertain visitors, professional work space, and parking or garage space.

9. *How do I learn to share space and responsibilities with non-relatives?*

   When residents contribute personal possessions for use in shared space, it supports everyone's sense of belonging. Additionally, sharing household chores and decision-making responsibilities tends to help people feel they are a necessary part of the group. Remember, it will take time for the members of your group to get to know one another and form the camaraderie most are seeking when entering into this type of arrangement—but, eventually it will happen.

10. *How will decisions about daily life be made?*

    If the group forms preliminary, flexible guidelines for decision making, resolving these issues will not be a problem. Be creative when establishing guidelines. There are no binding rules to doing this, and you can change them as you go along. Those who live together in a shared housing situation agree that it is best to establish house rules regarding the use of common space, meals to be shared, the distribution of shopping and cleaning chores, a guest policy, and methods for handling the illness of a member. Whenever possible, decisions should be made by consensus. Provide time at least once a month for house meetings.

Age-Segregated Programs in the United States

Subsidized and Congregate Living Facilities

The first public housing project specifically for older people was built in San Antonio, Texas, in the early 1960s. Since then, similar high-rise units financed and subsidized by the Department of Housing and Urban Development (HUD) have been developed in almost every community in the country. Unfortunately, since the 1980s there has been a drastic reduction in the number of new complexes due to budget constraints.

Only elderly persons who meet certain income guidelines qualify for this type of housing, which has been built by various non-profit and for-profit organizations, as well as public housing authorities with HUD financing. Residents must continue to qualify for public housing on an annual basis, and then pay 30% of their monthly income for rent.

Transportation services are important for senior housing residents.

Due to government cutbacks and the growing elderly population, subsidized housing arrangements are becoming more difficult to find. Additionally, many residents have lived in these units for over 10 to 15 years, and these housing developments have failed to meet many residents' increasing needs for social- and health-related services.

Experimental HUD Programs

In response to this void, HUD and a major private foundation have initiated a series of modest programs in several states to research and develop a range of social service programs that will provide support services for residents with health and mobility problems. Even though most communities have meal delivery and transportation services for shopping and medical appointments, such programs are often overwhelmed as they try to meet the needs of many on a tight budget. It is believed that frailer residents of subsidized housing units could benefit greatly from an in-house coordinator of services as well as a general manager on the premises. The success of some of these experimental programs lies in the fact that they permit residents to remain in their apartments longer, fostering a continuing sense of well-being and independence.

Advantages

• Affordability for low-income older persons

Disadvantages

• Support services are lacking.

• Few facilities have completed federally mandated accessibility guidelines—such essentials as accessible pathways from parking lots to building entrances for residents in wheelchairs have not been installed.

State-Funded Programs

In recent years, several states have initiated state-funded programs to pay for the construction of 20- to 30-unit congregate housing facilities with a limited amount of support services. These approximately 700-square-foot apartments are either a studio or one-bedroom design. Similar to the HUD subsidized units, applicants must meet certain income guidelines for admission to the program, and then they will also qualify for a monthly rental subsidy. In addition to weekly housekeeping services, an evening meal is provided by the facility in a common dining room. Several other common spaces are situated throughout the facility, including a recreation room. Staffing is kept to a minimum, but many facilities have some support services such as a weekly visit to the facility by a nurse or doctor.

Congregate housing with limited support services is provided by some state-funded programs.

Advantages

- Cost is low.
- Availability of some support services may postpone one's entry into a skilled nursing facility.
- Organization of successful tenant associations or social programs can promote interaction among residents.

Disadvantages

- Units are small.
- Lack of a social director to organize events may make residents feel isolated from one another.

Adult Retirement and Leisure Communities

These communities are usually housing developments designed primarily for adults over a certain age (usually 55). Many such developments are located in warm climate areas like Scottsdale, Arizona; Fort Lauderdale and Miami, Florida; western North Carolina; and Palm Springs, California. Perhaps the most well-

The first adult retirement community was in Sun City, Arizona.

known of these communities was the first one, Sun City, located outside of Phoenix.

Establishing residency in one of these environments is quite easy. Essentially, one buys a home in the development under a standard real estate arrangement. Units range in size from small one- or two-bedroom apartments, single-story homes, or condominiums to larger three- and four-bedroom homes with full yards. Prices vary as well, and one can pay anywhere from $25,000 to over $500,000. Cost is generally consistent with the type of community you will live in, and they can range from low-cost developments to resort-like facilities with private golf courses, tennis courts, club houses, and swimming pools. Annual maintenance fees and recreation fees may also be a part of the purchase agreement. In some cases, you can rent your residence on either a short- or long-term basis.

Advantages

- Relatively inexpensive housing, especially when compared to the equivalent apartment or house in the general community

- Residents relatively the same age and from similar backgrounds

- Planned activities and special events

- Recreational facilities such as clubhouses, pools, golf courses, and tennis courts

- Security and crime control

Disadvantages

- Location may be distant from cities because of the size and layout of the community.

- Emphasis on group recreational activities can limit privacy.

- Uniformity of surroundings

- Limited exposure to anyone but other retirees
- Houses or apartments often small
- Strict rules regarding visitation of young children
- Lack of intergenerational dimensions
- Limited accommodations for those with accessibility problems
- No formal arrangements for assisted living, support services or long-term care, although some of these communities are striving to become more service-oriented

Service-Oriented Retirement Communities

This type of community is designed to reduce caregiving responsibilities for residents who might have previously depended on family members or friends. In the service-oriented community, individuals are provided with a range of services from basic housekeeping and meals to full-time medical care. Aimed primarily at middle- to upper-income retirees, cost of living in such an environment varies and depends on the number of services provided as well as the location and type of facility one chooses.

The three most common types of service-oriented living environments are:

- Rental retirement communities
- Assisted-living facilities
- Continuing care, or lifecare communities

It is important to note that these terms are general designations and are sometimes used interchangeably. Each, however, has various different services to offer.

Rental Retirement Communities

These communities may be operated by either non-profit or for-profit organizations. Some offer only housing and recreation facilities, while others are more service oriented and provide housekeeping and on-site medical care.

A typical rental retirement facility consists of a three-story apartment building with approximately 150 living units clustered around a common area with dining room, auditorium, library, and sometimes a bank and a small post office. Usually located on a large site, these facilities offer a variety of social and

Some rental retirement communities offer services such as housekeeping, recreation, and on-site medical care.

activity programs organized by a staff social director. Free transportation to shopping areas and medical appointments is customarily provided. There is full security, a weekly cleaning service, and an individual medical monitoring service in each apartment. The latter may consist of a pull alarm in each room or a simple checklist system on the door or mailbox that indicates whether a resident has gotten up that day and is feeling okay. An evening meal is generally provided in the dining room, and residents can prepare breakfast and lunch in their own kitchenettes. Financing can be either a monthly rental fee with an additional charge for services utilized or apartments may be purchased outright with monthly fees charged for additional services. Purchase prices generally start at $100,000, with monthly fees of up to $1,500. One complex in Connecticut offers a 900-square-foot apartment for $116,000, with a monthly fee of $689. An additional $300 per month in fees is required for a second person in the unit.

Another Connecticut complex, the Gables in Farmington, is an excellent example of a state-of-the-art rental retirement community. Owned and managed by Advantage Health Corporation of Boston, the three-story apartment building has 174 living units including a ground floor dining room, lounges, library, auditorium, beauty/barber shop, and activity room. Among the 174 units are 14 apartments adapted for an assisted-living program. Located on a 20-acre, naturally landscaped site surrounded by a lake, the Gables is 120 miles from Boston and 90 miles from New York City.

Various social and activity programs are coordinated by a staff social director and tenants' association. A daily evening meal, free transportation to shopping areas and medical appointments, full security, housekeeping, and monitoring services are also provided. Private nursing, home health, and companion services are also available on a fee-for-service basis. Pets are allowed.

Locating this type of a community in a college setting achieves an urban environment that may be desirable. Examples include Clemson Downs in Clemson, South Carolina near Clemson University, a community on the campus of Eckerd College near St. Petersburg in Florida, and a new intergenerational facility on the campus of Syracuse University housing 400 older people and 750 graduate students and their families.

Advantages

- Similar to adult retirement and leisure communities, but more sensitive to the needs of residents with health and mobility problems

Disadvantages

- High cost
- Age segregation
- Distance from urban areas, although more major cities are developing these complexes
- Personal limitations imposed by community

Assisted-Living facilities

Assisted-living facilities are residential care facilities for independent seniors with multiple needs, including slight to moderate physical disabilities and cognitive impairment. Residents receive 24-hour supervision and assistance with the basic activities of daily living, including meal preparation, housekeeping, transportation, and recreation. The staff also provide general health or nursing assistance on an as-needed, intermittent basis. This includes reminders for or assistance in taking medical prescriptions and daily or weekly visits by a physician. Residents typically have their own private apartments and share public spaces with others.

This six-bed residential care facility offers 24-hour supervision and assistance with the basic activities of daily living.

Specific names of these facilities often depend on local nomenclature and various state regulations. Because of this, you may have heard such facilities referred to as:

- Adult homes or board and care homes
- Personal care homes
- Residential care facilities

Perhaps one of the most noticeable advantages of an assisted-living situation is the ability to provide care for individuals with Alzheimer's disease. These facilities provide maximum independence for these people, but at the same time offer round-the-clock assistance to control wandering and other behaviors that make it difficult for a person afflicted with this condition to function in his or her own home, even with the help of a spouse or other family member.

Advantages

- Allows an individual to maintain a greater level of independence than a standard skilled nursing facility

- Meals, baths, toileting, and other support services provided as needed

- Reduction of stress on spouses and family members who may have been previously caring for the individual at home

- Full range of nursing and medical care is available if needed

- Security and companionship

Disadvantages

- High cost and limited Medicare reimbursement (however, some states such as Oregon have obtained Medicaid waivers for low-income individuals)

- Lack of privacy

- Independence, while encouraged, not completely achievable

Continuing Care Retirement Communities

Continuing care retirement communities (CCRCs) offer a wide array of services, ranging from independent living to complete skilled nursing care. The majority of the CCRCs are operated by non-profit or religious organizations, but hotel chains such as Marriott and Hyatt are moving into this industry and, with other large private developers, now operate nearly one–third of all facilities nationwide. Most CCRCs offer a variety of contract options. Commonly these include:

Continuing care retirement communities offer services from independent living to skilled nursing care.

- *All-inclusive or full-service contract.* This is often called a life-care contract and is guaranteed by paying an entrance fee. Although you do not own the residence, the facility you are moving into contracts with you to care for you for life, even if you will eventually require full-time skilled nursing care. Entrance fees vary, but usually range from $75,000 to $200,000. An option offered by some communities includes a refund of a portion of the entrance fee if you leave the facility. Monthly service fees ranging from $700 to $2,000 are usually charged. This fee covers all services including housekeeping, meals, custodial care, assistance in bathing or dressing, and recreational and social activities.

- *Modified continuing care contract.* This type of contract is less costly than an all-inclusive one and offers fewer guaranteed medical services. Both entrance fees and monthly service fees are generally lower. A typical plan includes all housekeeping and meal services, but only some health services. Some of these contracts include an insurance option that will pay up to $40 per day toward nursing facility care if that becomes necessary.

- *A la carte services or fee-for-services contracts.* These contracts have options that allow you to pay for medical and personal services as you require them. Standard entrance and monthly fees are in the lowest range, and you are billed for the services you require as you use them.

The Church Home of Hartford, Inc., is an Episcopal-sponsored non-denominational, non-profit organization managed by Van Scoyoc Associates. Located in Bloomfield, Connecticut, this facility's Seabury Community consists of 37 cottages, 118 apartments, and a 109-room health center consisting of 49 congregate units, 30 assisted-living units, and 30 intermediate and skilled nursing units. The apartments are on three levels and are connected by closed hallways that lead to common areas which include a dining room, library, auditorium, classroom, and several other facilities. The four healthcare sections extend outward from the common area and surround a central courtyard.

A variety of social programs sponsored by an activities director and the tenants' association are offered. The full-service contract also provides one meal per day, free transportation to shopping areas and medical appointments, full security, housecleaning, and home health care as needed. Pets are allowed.

All-inclusive contract options are available with three different fee and refund schedules. These range from moderate entrance and monthly fees with a full refund minus 2% per month for 50 months to a higher entrance fee with a moderate monthly fee and a 67% refund at any time.

Like assisted-living facilities, CCRCs are ideal for middle- to upper-income individuals who are concerned about long-term care needs and do not want to move in with family members or worry about having to leave their home and go directly into a nursing facility in later years. Those living in these communities report a certain peace of mind associated with having their needs taken care of and not being dependent upon their children or other family members.

Advantages

- Access to medical services and guaranteed long-term care if one has contracted for it
- Security of knowing increased medical attention available within the community

Disadvantages

- Reduced privacy with a more regulated environment

- Distance from urban areas

- Age segregation

- Uncertainty about impact of inflation on medical expenses and monthly fees

- Risk of lost or reduced value of initial entrance fee if community experiences financial difficulty

International Models for Senior Living

Odense, Denmark—"The Self-Help Principle"

Perhaps the most exciting international example of a senior living environment is a program organized in the city of Odense, Denmark. Odense has a population of 172,000 people, of whom approximately 25,000 are over 65 years of age. This community has a long tradition of working with its older citizens to make their environment more "elder-friendly." The initial approach to this included establishing "self-help" as a principle in all activities in which seniors participated. The primary goal—consistent with the national government's goal of adding no more nursing facility beds after 1980—was to help the elderly remain in their own homes as long as possible.

In the late 1970s, Odense had only enough nursing facility beds for 6% of its senior citizen population and sheltered hous-

This community in Odense, Denmark offers group activities.

ing for only 2% of the same group. A few years earlier, a study of 2,000 elderly individuals was conducted in which they were regularly visited at home by nurses who gave them advice and guidance, as well as practical help to facilitate independent living. As a result, these 2,000 people, versus a control group of unvisited elderly people, had significantly fewer requests for nursing facility beds and were generally able to live longer in their own homes because of these visits.

At the beginning of the 1980s, Odense had 1,450 geriatric beds, 500 sheltered homes with some support services, 100 collective or shared facilities, and 1,200 pensioner or "elder-friendly" homes. The city government determined that these numbers would permanently remain at these levels and that 1,800 additional "elder-friendly" homes would be built for the elderly. By 1988, 908 of the homes, through cooperation of the city planning department and the social and welfare departments, had been erected. In general, few of the city's seniors objected to moving from their own homes to an "elder-friendly" home, as long as they could remain in their own neighborhoods. Overall, these new homes were more physically accessible and usable for older people and were located closer to shopping and public transportation.

Under the "self-help" principle, the older residents of Odense were encouraged to help one another perform various everyday tasks. Work chains were developed in which an older man might do carpentry work for an older woman in exchange for sewing or mending. Sighted seniors might read personal correspondence for visually impaired individuals in exchange for produce from their gardens. These work chains were organized through a group of clubs. By 1981, Odense had over 155 clubs all run by its seniors who developed their own cooperative work projects. Senior centers with kitchens and various social services were also developed. Many of these were built by retirees at considerable savings to the city. Located next to elderly housing, these senior centers not only provided a place for socializing, but also a facility where nursing services and preventive medical care could be accessed. In addition, the city opened several adult day care centers for seniors needing less care than that offered by a full-time, around-the-clock nursing facility. The number of users of these facilities rose from 364 in 1981, to 594 in 1986, with 100 people on a waiting list. To publicize these various programs, the local welfare department sponsors a quarterly magazine which relies on senior volunteers for most of its articles. Local officials often speak on elderly policy, and all home programs are coordinated locally by the area welfare office.

Odense has also expanded its active homecare program which has become considerably easier to implement due to the increase in the number of "elder-friendly" homes. Nursing assistance is currently provided for 5,000 citizens, of whom 300 receive 24-hour care. By 1988, the city employed 100 home helpers and 136 home nurses. A 24-hour personal medical paging program to contact emergency medical professionals in the event of an acute health problem was also instituted. Local physicians and hospitals cooperated closely with this program to avoid unnecessary hospitalizations and arrange earlier releases. Statistics show that since 1987, Odense uses significantly fewer hospital beds for an increasing population of seniors. Instead of building two additional nursing facilities in the 1980s, the city built 28 collective homes with plans for another 160 "elder-friendly" homes in groups of four or five, each with its own activity center.

When seniors are encouraged to be more independent, the quality of their lives can be greatly improved.

The city of Odense is well on the way to meeting its goals established in the 1980s. As the "self-help" philosophy continues to encourage the city's seniors to help themselves and their neighbors, this program becomes even more cost-effective for the city while improving the quality of life of its older residents.

Adelaide, Australia—"Mission's Aldersgate Village"

A similar philosphy is exemplified by the Mission, an organization that has operated an elderly housing facility in Australia since 1944. Providing accommodations for over 400 elderly people, Aldersgate Village's architectural design and medical support services were similar to a hospital facility. In recent years, the management determined that the facility was fostering dependency rather than independence, with residents viewing themselves as patients instead of independent adults with support needs. A new philosophy was developed to address emotional, spiritual, social, and intellectual needs, and a new facility was built to foster independence and a sense of "home" instead of "institution."

The new facility resembles a large home with separate living areas for each resident. A resident is allowed to individualize the interior design and function with this "home" setting as he or she would at home, entertaining guests in privacy. Support and healthcare services are individualized to meet each resident's needs while fostering an appropriate level of independent living and socialization. For example, a study shared by residents and staff replaces the typical nursing station, which helps to reduce the residents' perception of themselves as "client" to the staff's role of "caregiver." Additionally, a restaurant has replaced the conventional central dining area, further reinforcing a sense of independence and self-worth.

The Mobile Home Option

Presently, there are approximately 4 million mobile homes in the United States providing housing for nearly 8.5 million people, of whom more than half are retired. At a median cost of $30,000 for a new mobile home, these units represent the least expensive type of private housing available. Even if property is included with the unit in a mobile home park, the cost is still low, ranging from $34,000 to $62,000. Monthly fees including water, garbage pickup, and the use of recreational facilities can be an additional $100 to $600.

A typical mobile home measures 14 feet by 65 feet, although some are larger and quite luxurious, equipped with all modern appliances and wall-to-wall carpeting. Many units, like the large Winnebago, can be used to travel around the country; however, these large vehicles are inefficient gas-guzzlers and barely achieve 5 miles per gallon. Trailer parks often have paved roads, swimming pools, and other amenities and may be "closed" (homes must be purchased on-site from the developer) or "open" (residents can purchase or rent space and move in with their own mobile homes).

Individuals considering this option are advised to rent a unit first and use it for several vacations before making any type of permanent living arrangements. Further information on mobile home living can be obtained from the Manufactured Housing Institute, 1745 Jefferson Davis Highway, Suite 511, Arlington,

Virginia, 22201 (703/558-0400) or from the various mobile home manufacturers such as Winnebago and Air Stream.

Advantages

- Relatively low cost

- Some units able to be driven around the country

Disadvantages

- Limited space and hard to modify for accessibility

- Lack of privacy

- Locations often in isolated areas away from shopping, police and fire protection, and medical care

- Car often a necessity

- Some parks very restrictive, prohibiting pets and children

Elder Cottage Housing Opportunity

Elder Cottage Housing Opportunity, or ECHO housing, is usually a prefabricated house delivered by truck and placed in a side or rear yard of an adult child or other family member's home. Such units generally cost about $15,000 to $20,000, and contain one bedroom, a living room, a fully equipped kitchen, full bath, heater, washer, and dryer. Moving into such a unit provides an older person with a continuing sense of independence as well as the opportunity for informal visits and shared meals with nearby family. It can also be a mutually helpful arrangement if the older family member can care for grandchildren in exchange for receiving help with house-

An Elder Cottage allows an older person both independence from and closeness with nearby family.
Courtesy of HomeCare Suites, Birmingham, Michigan

hold chores and shopping. A similar approach involves the construction of a caregiver or accessory apartment in a single family house.

Strict zoning laws in many communities, however, have greatly restricted the development of more ECHO housing in the United States. Towns favoring the single-family housing design protest that the placement of ECHO units lowers property values, raises the cost of area social services thus increasing taxes, and aesthetically spoils the appearance of residential neighborhoods. Builders in various states have presented their cases to local zoning boards and have been able to obtain exemptions for specific individuals assuming they will be the only occupants of these units. California is one state that has passed legislation allowing such cottages, providing they are attractive and fit into the design of a neighborhood and can be easily dismantled and removed when they are no longer in use.

More information on ECHO Housing can be obtained by writing to HomeCare Suites Inc., 805 East Maple Road, Suite 310, Birmingham, Michigan 48009.

Advantages

- Low cost
- Potential for mutually beneficial "chore-exchange" arrangement between older resident and property owner's family

Disadvantages

- Zoning problems
- May need to be removed when no longer occupied by elders

References

McCamant, Katharine, and Charles Durret. *Cohousing: A Contemporary Approach to Housing Ourselves.* Berkeley, Calif.: Habitat Press, 1988.

Porcino, Jane. *Living Longer and Better: Adventures in Community Housing in the Second Half of Life.* New York: Continuum Publishing, 1991.

Regnier, Victor. *Assisted-Living Housing for the Elderly: Design Innovations from the United States and Europe.* New York: Van Nostrand Reinhold, 1994.

Suggested Readings

Boyer, Richard, and David Savagean. *Places Rated Almanac: Your Guide to Finding the Best Places to Live in America.* New York: Rand McNally, 1985.

Dychtwald, Ken, and Joe Flower. *Age Wave.* Los Angeles: Jeremy P. Tarcher, 1989.

Huttman, Elizabeth D. *Social Services for the Elderly.* New York: The Free Press, 1985.

Mogensen, Tove, and Lisa Birn. *Odense Municipality Elderly Policy.* Odense, Denmark: Social Welfare Department, Municipality of Odense, 1988.

Chapter Three

Evaluating Your Resources

Financial Resources

Before going any further in this book, you have to ask some very fundamental questions about your housing choice: How much will it cost? How can I afford that? What should I know about senior services in the community? In short, it is time to conduct a thorough analysis of your financial resources and how they will affect your long-term planning.

You will need about 80% of what you earn while working to live comfortably when you retire. Getting your home fixed up or making other living arrangements prior to retirement, before the vagaries of old age, can help ensure that you have that kind of money.

Library shelves are full of books identifying the benefits and limitations of various retirement plans, such as IRAs and 401 (k)s. In this chapter we will concentrate primarily on financial planning techniques that can help with your place of residence whether you decide to modify your present home, build a new accessible one, or move into a retirement community.

It is important to understand that our recommendations should not replace an individualized financial and estate plan developed by an attorney, accountant, financial planner, or trust officer. These suggestions, however, can help you organize your financial data to help determine how much will be available for housing, as well as how long-term care insurance may influence your planning.

Family Assets

It is important to understand the basic elements of a financial plan. This is a simple "What am I worth and what will I live on?" analysis, including a review of your life and health insurance data, especially your planned Medicare and supplemental health insurance policies, long-term care insurance, property and casualty insurance, your investment plan, and anticipated taxes. The latter would include your anticipated property, state, and federal taxes during your retirement years. By completing this type of analysis you will know how much you can spend to modify your present house, to sell the house and purchase a new universally designed home, or to contract for admission to a Continuing Care Retirement Community (CCRC). Whether you have long-term care insurance that includes coverage of home-care is also essential for comparing the costs of homecare versus what might be available in a CCRC. This is especially important because some CCRCs include a resident-owned long-term care policy as part of their life care contract.

Analyzing Family Finances

The following worksheet offers important tools for identifying realistic options. Based on a form developed by Barry Hibben, a San Francisco stockbroker, it is simple to use and can help you determine your available funds for housing modifications or purchasing a new, more accessible home. To make the Hibben process easier to understand, we have completed the form using a fictitious couple—Andrew and Samantha Jones—based on their circumstances 5 years before retirement.

A family without sufficient resources to cover a major modification might want to explore reverse equity mortgages, a new technique that has been used successfully to unlock the major assets many older families have in their home. (Refer to the discussion later in this chapter.)

Financial Analysis of Andrew and Samantha Jones

I. **To determine their net worth the Joneses first calculate and list all of their assets:**

1. *Current Assets*

a)	Cash	$ 2,000.
b)	Checking/money-market accounts	15,000.
c)	Savings accounts	25,000.
d)	Insurance cash values	75,000.
e)	Stocks, bonds, mutual funds	300,000.
	Subtotal	*$ 417,000.*

2. *Fixed Assets*

a)	Home or residence	$ 250,000.
b)	Any other real estate	75,000.
c)	Car, truck, van, etc.	40,000.
d)	Furniture	50,000.
e)	Valuable jewelry	10,000.
	Subtotal	*$ 425,000.*

3. *Deferred Assets*

a)	IRA, Keogh, pension plans	$ 250,000.
b)	Heirlooms and antiques	20,000.
c)	Miscellaneous	10,000.
	Subtotal	*$ 280,000.*
Total Assets		*$1,122,000.*

Next, they total their liabilities:

1. *Current Liabilities*

a)	Credit card debt	$ 4,000.
b)	Auto debt	20,000.
c)	Annual property taxes	1,500.
d)	Utility bills (12 months)	3,000.
e)	Other debts due this year	2,500.
	Subtotal	*$ 31,000.*

2.   *Long-Term Liabilities*

    a)   Home mortgage $ 50,000.

    b)   Vacation home mortgage   20,000.

    c)   Personal loans   10,000.

    d)   Student loans   13,000.

    Subtotal $ 93,000.

Total Liabilities $ 124,000.

By subtracting their total liabilities from their total assets, the Joneses determine that their net worth is $907,000.

Total Assets	$ 1,122,000.
Total Liabilities	– $ 124,000.
Net Worth	= $ 907,000.

II.   The Joneses now calculate what they will live on. They list their annual income as follows:

1.   *Current Annual Income*

    a)   Salary, bonus (Andrew) $ 70,000.

    b)   Self-employed income (Samantha)   20,000.

    c)   Real estate income (net after taxes)   -

    d)   Dividends from all sources   5,000.

    e)   Interest (bonds, bank, or money-market accounts)   10,000.

2.   *Potential Annual Income*

    a)   Life insurance settlement options   -

    b)   Social Security income   -

    c)   Annuities   -

    d)   Keogh or IRA distributions   -

Total Annual Income $ 105,000.

They list their annual expenses as follows:

1.   *Fixed Expenses*

    a)   Housing (rent, repairs and maintenance, condo fees, etc.) $ 4,000.

    b)   Home mortgage   18,000.

c)	Car loan	2,400.
d)	Home equity loan	-
e)	Real estate taxes	1,500.
f)	Personal property taxes	1,000.
g)	Income taxes, Social Security payments	20,000.
h)	Food	5,000.
i)	Clothing	3,000.
j)	Transportation (auto maintenance, fuel, etc.)	500.
k)	Annual medical/dental expenses (unreimbursed)	2,000.
l)	Insurance:	
	Medical	1,400.
	Medicare Part B	-
	Long-term care	2,500.
	Life	1,000.
	Auto, property, and casualty	1,500.
	Subtotal	*$ 63,800.*
2.	*Discretionary Expenses*	
a)	Vacations	$ 6,000.
b)	Recreation/entertainment	5,000.
c)	Contributions/gifts	2,000.
d)	Household furnishings	1,500.
e)	Education	-
f)	Savings, IRA	5,000.
g)	Investments, other	10,000.
	Subtotal	*$ 29,500.*
	Total Annual Expenses	*$ 93,300.*

The Jones' calculations reveal that they have a surplus of $11,700.

Total Annual Income		*$ 105,000.*
Total Annual Expenses		*– $ 93,300.*
Surplus		*= $ 11,700.*

If the Joneses decide to sell their principal residence (which has an assured gain in value in excess of $125,000) they will benefit from the one-time $125,000 capital gains exclusion allowed couples who are age 55 and older. As a result of this exclusion, they will not have to pay any income taxes on this amount of capital gains.

On the basis of their analysis, the Joneses determine that they have sufficient funds for a $40,000 modification to their primary residence and another $5,000 to plan the work on their vacation home. The small mortgage balance on their primary residence would allow them to use a home equity loan rather than any of their other assets for the work. This loan could then be repaid over time using investment income. Should the Joneses decide to build a new home, they could sell their current house, avoid the capital gains tax on the $125,000 lifetime exclusion, and invest the funds in the new house.

Financial Analysis Worksheet

I.　What Am I Worth?

ASSETS: To determine what you are worth, you first need to calculate and list all of your assets—current, fixed, and deferred.

1.　*Current Assets*

　　a)　Cash _____

　　b)　Checking/money-market accounts _____

　　c)　Savings accounts _____

　　d)　Insurance cash values _____

　　e)　Stocks, bonds, mutual funds _____

　　Subtotal _____

2.　*Fixed Assets*

　　a)　Home or residence _____

　　b)　Any other real estate _____

　　c)　Car, truck, van, etc. _____

　　d)　Furniture _____

　　e)　Valuable jewelry _____

　　Subtotal _____

3.　*Deferred Assets*

　　a)　IRA, Keogh, pension plans _____

　　b)　Heirlooms and antiques _____

　　c)　Miscellaneous _____

　　Subtotal _____

Total Assets _____

LIABILITIES: Now that you have the estimated value of your assets, you need to total your liabilities. Liabilities are usually of two types: current and long term.

1.　*Current Liabilities*

　　a)　Credit card debt _____

　　b)　Auto debt _____

　　c)　Annual property taxes _____

    d)   Utility bills (12 months)   _____

    e)   Other debts due this year   _____

    Subtotal   _____

2.   *Long-Term Liabilities*

    a)   Home mortgage   _____

    b)   Vacation home mortgage   _____

    c)   Personal loans   _____

    d)   Student loans   _____

    Subtotal   _____

Total Liabilities   _____

NET WORTH: By subtracting the total of your liabilities from the total of your assets, you now know what you are worth. But, don't forget that the value of assets can change from one day to the next, so the net worth calculation is really only accurate for today.

Total Assets   _____

Total Liabilities   −   _____

Net Worth   =   _____

II.   What Will I Live On?

Having established your net worth, it is now easy to answer the question, "What will I live on?"

ANNUAL INCOME: First you need to list the income you receive from all sources, both current and potential.

1.   *Current Annual Income*

    a)   Salary, plus any bonus   _____

    b)   Other income   _____

    c)   Real estate income (net after taxes)   _____

    d)   Dividends from all sources   _____

    e)   Interest (bonds, bank, or money-market accounts)   _____

    Subtotal   _____

2.   *Potential Annual Income*

    a)   Life insurance settlement options   _____

b)   Social Security income   _____

c)   Annuities   _____

d)   Keogh or IRA distributions   _____

Subtotal   _____

Total Annual Income   _____

ANNUAL EXPENSES: Next, you need to list all the ways you spend your income.

The following categories cover the usual expenditures, but you may have others, so be sure to add anything that is a regular expenditure for you. Remember, you are listing annual expenses, so if the monthly figures vary, average the monthly and multiply by 12.

Annual expenses fall into one of two general categories: fixed or discretionary.

1.   *Fixed Expenses*

a)   Housing (rent, repairs and maintenance, condo fees, etc.)   _____

b)   Home mortgage   _____

c)   Home equity loan   _____

d)   Other debt repayment (car, credit card)   _____

e)   Real estate taxes   _____

f)   Personal property taxes   _____

g)   Income taxes, Social Security   _____

h)   Food   _____

i)   Clothing   _____

j)   Transportation (auto maintenance, fuel, etc.)_____

k)   Annual medical/dental expenses (unreimbursed)   _____

l)   Insurance: _____

Medical   _____

Medicare Part B   _____

Long-term care   _____

Life   _____

Auto, property, and casualty   _____

Subtotal   _____

2.   *Discretionary Expenses*

    a)   Vacations   _____

    b)   Recreation/entertainment   _____

    c)   Contributions/gifts   _____

    d)   Household furnishings   _____

    e)   Education   _____

    f)   Savings, IRA   _____

    g)   Investments, other   _____

    Subtotal   _____

Total Annual Expenses   _____

By subtracting total expenses from total income, you now have the answer to the question, "What will I live on?"

Total Annual Income   _____

Total Annual Expenses   –   _____

Surplus (+) or deficit (-)   =   _____

III.   Where Do I Go From Here?

It is now clear by how much your income exceeds or falls short of your expenses. A surplus can be programmed for additional savings or other uses. A deficit can be made up by careful planning. A few suggestions may help:

1.   What you will have for retirement income is largely a function of: (a) Retirement benefits (pension and Social Security) plus (b) Income from investments (real estate, stocks and bonds, annuities, etc.). By utilizing the calculations outlined here, it is easy to estimate what that income will be.

2.   On both the income and expenditure lists you may find categories that do not apply to you, and you may add others that we don't list here. The items should be "customized" to suit your situation.

3.   It's a good idea to recalculate the figures each year; this will help you to keep track of the numbers you need, thus making the second calculations more accurate.

This worksheet has been adapted from a form developed by Barry Hibben of Hibinfo, Mill Valley, CA. It is used with his permission.

The Caregiver: Potential Financial Benefits

Accommodations for an in-home caregiver should be considered as you plan your own housing. You may find you have a niece or nephew who, for free rent, will help you with activities such as cooking, shopping, or yard work. Alternatively you might plan for a live-in nurse's aide who could help with daily hygiene and nutritious meals.

Your preference depends on current and potential future needs, but you should include a caregiver in your financial analysis. One consideration, for example, is whether to build a separate (accessory) apartment for a future caregiver—either for full rental or for rental at a reduced fee in exchange for services. Such estimates will be helpful in deciding what to spend on modifications or on a new house. (It should be noted that this question must be reviewed with your local zoning and planning staff.) Usually, an architect or builder can provide the necessary guidance; however, as we stated in Chapter 2, a team approach, including the recommendations of a occupational therapist, should be considered when possible.

Long-Term Care Insurance

Long-term care, the ongoing custodial or skilled assistance required by individuals with chronic illness or disability, is another important factor to be considered when evaluating your finances. This level of care consists of help with activities of daily living such as eating, bathing, and dressing, and it is usually precipitated by a medical condition such as arthritis, a stroke, heart attack, or a cognitive impairment like Alzheimer's disease. A disability may also develop gradually as in the case of blindness.

Long-term care can be very expensive. In some cases it can be as much as $30,000 to $60,000 per year for nursing home costs alone. Long-term care can quickly drain the life savings of even the wealthiest individual and should be a major consideration in your planning. Approximately 50% of the cost of long-term care nationwide is paid by individuals, with the balance coming mainly from Medicaid (often requiring a couple to deplete or "spend down" their assets to achieve eligibility) (Peterson, 1988).

Long-term care insurance is available for care received both in the home and in a nursing facility.

Insurance company statistics point out that 43% of those over the age of 65 will need some long-term care either at home or in a nursing facility. Furthermore, with inflation factored in at a 5% rate, the average daily rate for a nursing home in 1990 ($100) would reach $265 per day by 2010 (Polniaszek, 1992).

Medicare pays only 2% of the national total cost of long-term care, and it only comes into play for a short time after a hospitalization (Peterson, 1988). Most knowledgeable observers doubt that Medicare coverage of long-term care will be increased in the future, especially with the rapidly increasing costs of Medicaid.

With the potential risk that long-term care needs will wipe out the savings of most middle-income families, long-term care insurance is becoming an increasingly important option for most families. The probability of a need for some long-term care increases from 1% for those between the ages 65 and 74, to 6% for those age 75 to 84, and to 22% for those 85 and over (U.S. Senate, Special Committee on Aging, 1989). Insurance company statistics point out that 43% of those over the age of 65 will need some long-term care either at home or in a nursing facility. Furthermore, with inflation factored in at a 5% rate, the average daily rate for a nursing home in 1990 ($100) would reach $265 per day by 2010 (Polniaszek, 1992).

Long-term care is also closely connected to housing needs. Considering that in most cases family members do some of the caregiving, home-based care is usually less expensive than nursing facility care. More important, most of us want to stay home, if at all possible. A 1990 study by the American Association of Retired Persons (AARP) documents that 86% of seniors prefer staying at home. Thus if your home is modified or you move into an "elder-friendly" new home, it will be easier to function comfortably in a supportive physical environment. Such a home also will make it easier for the caregiver to carry out required tasks. For example, widening corridors and interior doors enables a caregiver to maneuver a family member more easily through the house in a wheelchair. Many other modifications and products are available to help create a more accommodating house and reduce the risks of falling and other accidents while improving accessibility for services required in the home. It is of interest to note that some insurance companies are beginning to recognize the positive impact of home accessibility on homecare. As a result, these companies offer reimbursement for such home modifications as lowering counters in kitchens for qualifying policy holders.

Elders function more easily in a supportive physical environment.

Because most long-term care policies are usually activated by physical impairments affecting two or three activities of daily living (eating, grooming, dressing) or by cognitive impairment, insurance will pay either for home-based or care in a nursing facility. Many professionals recommend that families purchase homecare benefits equal to those for nursing facility care. Although one can still buy nursing facility-only policies, regulators are now requiring that each company offer both home-based and nursing facility coverage either as a comprehensive policy or with homecare riders. For example, in Connecticut two companies now offer a total long-term coverage policy at approximately $100 per day up to a maximum of $200,000. The owner, if qualified, can use this coverage for either home-based care or nursing facility care.

Unfortunately, many policyholders are not aware of this development, and a major company reports that its total sales still run 25% nursing home with homecare riders and 75% nursing home only. This is probably due to higher costs for the homecare coverage, but industry indicators suggest a stronger market for homecare in the future, which argues for either comprehensive policies or a higher percentage of coverage devoted to homecare. As reported in *Health Progress*, a 1989 study suggests that "long-term care used to be synonymous with nursing homes. Today it includes homecare and community services, and tomorrow it will mean a continuum of care that incorporates supportive housing and preventative services. Senior housing of all types will be in especially great demand."

The Costs

Because both home-based and nursing facility care insurance become increasingly expensive as you grow older, it can make a sizeable financial difference to purchase this insurance at a younger age. For example, a Teachers Insurance Association of America (TIAA) policy paying $100 per day for nursing facility benefits and $50 per day for home and adult day care benefits with an inflation protection option and a lifetime benefit maximum of $255,000 costs $1,215 per year if purchased at age 60. By the age of 75, a similar policy would cost $3,750 per year. Furthermore, few policies are issued after age 84, and as one grows older the odds of not passing a medical examination to qualify for the policy increase.

Other desirable features of long-term care insurance include guaranteed renewable-for-life policies, no prior hospitalization required (especially important for homecare), specific coverage for Alzheimer's disease and other forms of irreversible dementia, adult day care, and respite care.

What is important to remember is that long-term care insurance, especially policies with significant if not equal amounts for homecare, is a major factor in evaluating the benefits of investing in home modification or a new home. Policies usually pay a specific amount per day. A home environment that is modified for a person with disabilities can make it easier for the caregiver. The policy's adult day care and respite features also reduce substantially the strain on family members as well as on paid caregivers.

Continuing Care Retirement Community Contracts and Long-Term Care Insurance

The entry fee and monthly costs of a CCRC basically pay for the long-term care contract that these facilities offer. In other words, when you pay your entry fee (usually a minimum of $100,000) and the monthly fee, you are paying for the time you may have to spend in that part of the facility that provides nursing care. In essence, you are paying for the long-term care contract offered to you by the CCRC. In this regard, it is important that you understand clearly what you are getting for your money, including the number of days the CCRC will guarantee per year in the nursing facility without charging additional fees. Some offer lifetime guarantees; others only guarantee 90 days per year, and the resident must pay the private rate for the rest of his or her stay. Others will not provide this service free unless the resident gives up his or her apartment so that it can be made available to a new resident.

Funding Sources for Home Modification

Probably the best approach for financing home modifications is a home equity loan, especially if your current mortgage is low, minimal, or completely paid. For purchasing a new home, a standard mortgage usually makes the most sense, especially if the former house has been or will be sold. The homeowner, however, must have a regular source of income to satisfy mortgage payments.

If a homeowner is short of funds, there are a variety of ways to tap personal assets to finance the modifications. Among the most common of these are reverse mortgages, sale leaseback plans, and home equity loans.

Reverse Mortgages

Reverse mortgages allow older people to use the financial equity in their home without having to sell it. Simply put, the reverse mortgage allows a person to borrow from the home's equity or value. Although a conventional mortgage requires the owner to make regular loan payments consisting of interest and repayment of principal, a reverse mortgage gives the homeowner either a lump sum payment or regular periodic payments or "advances," similar to a line of credit. The loan proceeds can be used for any purpose, including, of course, modifications to the residence.

Interest rates on reverse mortgages vary greatly, and those offered by state and local governments are usually the lowest. Private lenders charge the most and often have high up-front charges for debt appraisal and loan insurance fees. Such fees, however, can often be added to the principal and paid out with the loan.

Unlike conventional mortgages, repayment of these loan advances is due only at the end of the loan period or when the person dies or sells the home. At the end of the loan period, the equity remaining in the home will be reduced substantially because the homeowner has already received it in the form of monthly advances and charged interest. During the period of the reverse mortgage, the homeowner retains the title to the house and is responsible for taxes and maintenance. There is a "limitation of liability" built into reverse mortgages that protects the other assets of the homeowner, because the amount of the loan that must be paid back is limited to the initial, assessed value of the home.

Reverse mortgages are also known as "rising debt" loans. They grow over time because the loan advances and the total amount of interest on these advances accumulates over the life of the loan. Unlike conventional mortgages this interest is not deductible until the mortgage is paid off, usually at the end of the loan period.

It is important to note that older homeowners have not enthusiastically taken part in the reverse mortgage programs. By the early 1990s, only about 155,000 of these mortgages had been closed despite high ownership rates, generally paid-up homes, and substantial home equity among seniors. A variety of reasons have been offered, including the complexity of the instrument, reluctance to tamper with one's major source of wealth, and the fact that these mortgages can be an expensive way to generate cash income, especially in periods of high interest rates. If a homeowner has other savings, it would be foolish to borrow money with this vehicle and receive no concurrent tax deduction for interest, while paying taxes on interest and dividend income from savings. On the other hand, couples with very little income or savings whose home is lien free would experience a considerable increase in their income, possibly permitting necessary improvements to their home.

Sale Leaseback Plans

With a sale leaseback, the home is sold to an investor, family member, or friend, and the original owner pays a monthly rent to remain in the home. Usually, the new owner guarantees the original owner an indefinite right to renew the lease annually. Responsibility for payment of property taxes and maintenance is negotiated between the parties.

The source of funds for home modification should be negotiated as well. Such factors as adding future value to the house should be discussed in the negotiation.

There are many facets to this type of transaction, and it has the potential for a variety of legal and financial consequences. It is important, therefore, for both parties to work with an attorney and evaluate all features carefully to be sure that they meet everyone's needs and objectives.

Reverse mortgages and sale leaseback plans are available to allow you to stay in your own home.

Home Equity Loans

Home equity loans are probably the most frequently utilized and desirable approaches for those wishing to make home modifications. Older home owners usually have minimal or no mortgage payments. This factor coupled with a high rate of home ownership by older adults makes such loans highly attractive to lending institutions.

The major risk of a home equity loan is that the lender may require loans to be paid back through a schedule of monthly payments; if not, the lender will foreclose on the home. If an older person does not have sufficient other income to repay the loan and uses such a loan to modify the home, he or she could be placed at considerable financial risk. Thus it is important for a family to examine its overall financial situation carefully and be sure that sufficient income is available to cover the interest and repayment of the loan.

Potential Financial Benefits of Adding a Separate Caregiver Apartment

One of the key benefits of home modification is the potential rental income from an accessory apartment. This potential has to be carefully calculated, and one must consider the extra property taxes and interest costs that a rented addition may create. It must also be recognized that such an addition will not be included in the value of the home for the over-55 capital gains exemption if one decides to sell the house at a later date.

Another important financial advantage of adding an accessory apartment is that it will allow an individual or couple to remain in the home and save the costs incurred and time spent selling a home. It also eliminates the psychological impact of leaving one's home.

Financial Aspects of Selling Your Current Home and Building a New One

If you decide to sell your current home and build a new one, there are many financial issues that must be examined. After completing an analysis of your finances, the next step is to obtain a realistic appraisal of the selling price of your current home and a solid budget for the new home. Factored into this comparison is the $125,000 one-time exclusion from capital gains tax for the sale of the house if the seller is age 55 or older.

Other local tax benefits should be investigated as well; for example, a veteran's assessment exemption and certain property tax reliefs for senior homeowners and renters are available in some areas based on income guidelines. These differ around the country but may substantially reduce property taxes for older residents in some communities.

You may find that there has been a sizable increase in the value of your home, especially if you have lived in it for 10 years or more. On the other hand, in some parts of the country, homes purchased in the 1950s and 1960s have not experienced such an appreciation.

Once your housing appraisal is in hand, you can determine how much of the money you expect to realize from the sale can be used as a down payment on the new house and how much of the cost must be covered with a new mortgage. The annual income you identified in the financial analysis of "What will I live on" will help determine if there is sufficient income available to cover the mortgage costs, taxes, and maintenance of the new house.

As with a home modification, another important consideration in purchasing a new house is the inclusion of an apartment either for rental to a tenant or eventually for rental at a reduced cost to a caregiver in exchange for specified services. If the new home does not have an apartment, is there a possibility that you can add one on if you choose?

Community Resources

Staying active by volunteering at a community museum can improve the quality of life.

An often overlooked aspect of housing decisions is the quality and extent of local community resources. We have all heard the story about the retired couple who moved to an attractive golfing retirement community with a home overlooking the first tee. Being quite well off financially, they were able to purchase one of the nicest homes in the community. Their initial and follow-up visits gave them a good sense of the attractiveness of the area but did not prepare them for the long drives just to reach a supermarket or major hospital. Essentially, this couple overlooked the all-important assessment of community resources that can be as important as a family's financial capabilities. Many of these resources have significant financial consequences, such as the availability of quality and fairly priced adult day care services, because without these services nearby, your costs to obtain them will increase substantially.

The number, types, and costs of community resources take on greater importance as we see our society placing greater value on quality of life issues. Your analysis of a community's resources should determine how close you are to medical services, both physician and hospital, as well as to local visiting nurse programs. You should also consider your proximity to shopping and community transportation services. For example, the beauty of a rural environment can very well become a severe burden for individuals requiring extensive medical and community services more often available or accessible in urban settings.

The standard services in a community should include:

- Accessible and available healthcare

- Multi-purpose senior centers that coordinate senior programs in a community

- Adult day care

- Continuing education or travel programs

- Volunteer programs for seniors

- Meals on Wheels

- Errand service for those who can no longer drive

- Chore services for homebound elderly

- Homemaker services

- Transportation for medical and personal needs

- Geriatric care management

- Telephone reassurance

- Friendly visitor program

Researching and Analyzing Senior Services

To evaluate the senior services in a community, you will need to conduct a detailed survey, focusing on the extent and quality of the services provided. The following questionnaire, Assessing Community Services, can assist you in this survey.

Let's return to the question of whether to modify your current home or move to a retirement community. Both choices have major financial implications that are difficult to assess because of variables such as health and healthcare. Now that more long-term care policies are comprehensive (i.e., cover both home-based and residential nursing care with interchangeable daily benefits), the financial benefits of remaining in a modified home may be greater. One may find that the cost of long-term care insurance plus the home modification cost is significantly less than the high entry fee and monthly cost of the CCRC. On

Assessing Community Services

The following questions can assist you in analyzing the senior services available in your community:

1.   *Does the town or city provide home-delivered meals? What are the guidelines for qualifying for the meal delivery? Is there a waiting list? What is the cost?*

2.   *What type of community transportation is available for homebound seniors? Can it be used for medical appointments as well as weekly shopping trips? What is the cost for accessing these services? What is the availability of these services?*

3.   *Is there an active senior center program in the community? It is recommended that you visit the center, discuss the program with the director, and obtain a calendar and other information on activities that are offered.*

4.   *Does the town or city offer home-chore or errand services for homebound seniors in their own homes? What agency provides these, what are the costs, and what is their availability?*

5.   *Are there community shopping services for homebound seniors? What agency provides these? What are the costs? What is the availability of these services?*

6.   *What opportunities are there in the community for lifelong learning? Is there an active program for such pursuits? What local junior college or high school programs offer continuing education courses? Does the local cable station offer such programs for homebound seniors to take part in? If not, is it planning to incorporate them in its local programming in the future?*

the other hand, the community may not have an adult day care center or reliable local transportation systems for older people who can no longer drive. These negative factors might offset the financial advantages of anticipated lower long-term care insurance costs as well as the psychological benefits of modifying and staying in one's home.

Knowing what a community offers in the way of senior services can often help a person make a decision about whether to continue to live there. For example, if a community has a wide range of well-run senior services, including an adult day care center and a senior center, an individual or a couple would be well served to modify the present home and buy comprehensive long-term care insurance. In such a scenario, these individuals can expect to remain in their own modified home for many more years and utilize the helpful services and programs available in their community. Should they reach a point where they must have skilled nursing care, they will be able to use their comprehensive long-term care policy for this purpose.

Availability and Accessibility of Healthcare

Things may not be always as they seem—so check carefully. Based on nine criteria (physicians per 100,000, teaching hospitals, medical schools, cardiac rehabilitation centers, air pollution, fluoridation, etc.), the number one metropolitan area in the country for healthcare and environment is New York City. (Boyer and Savageau, 1985). The unhealthiest place is not too far away—around Glens Falls, New York. It gets its low rating primarily because it offers nothing in the way of sophisticated care, and it costs a lot!

Some aspects of healthcare that you should explore when evaluating the resources of the community in which you may spend your retirement years include:

- *What is the daily cost of a hospital room?*
- *Can your personal physician take care of you or must it be a member of the hospital staff?*
- *What are the policies, in writing, on fees and coverage of emergency care?*
- *Are planned menus available for special diets?*
- *Is there an active, well-trained, and well-motivated staff; adequate support services and equipment?*
- *Are the facilities well maintained, attractive, and comfortable?*
- *Is there a variety of appealing activities for the elderly?*
- *What is the municipal budget for senior care activities?*
- *Does the hospital have access to high-tech diagnostic resources?*

The answers are by no means clear cut. You could answer "Yes" to all of the questions and still find yourself unhappy. Or you could answer "No" and find that the sound of ocean surf lulling you to sleep each night, the beauty of local foliage, or simply the presence of a group of friends who meet every afternoon for good talk, good tea, or other libation might counterbalance the negatives. But probably, experience shows, you will be better off with at least a few "Yesses" on your answer list. Plus, the rapid changes occurring in this area due to the growth of HMOs and managed care will make these questions even more difficult to answer.

Elder Services

The availability of elder services in a community is one financial consideration.

Researching elder services available in your community can be frustrating. Terminology is one of the problems, but providers and sources of funding differ also. For several years the federal Administration on Aging (AOA) has been involved in an effort to make the Area Agency on Aging the focal point of senior services. Even if all services are not coordinated by the nearest Area Agency on Aging, the agency usually has good information or a referral service to help you locate services and determine whether you are eligible. Once you have contacted the Area Agency, the next step is to check with your local senior center. These centers, of course, vary in services but, on balance, serve an important coordinating function. If you still find a significant gap in services, it might be wise to hire a professional geriatric care manager to help you through the labyrinth of senior services in your community. These are certified, trained professionals who are qualified to coordinate services. However, it is always important to check with responsible groups in a community such as the town social services department.

Individuals who work for large corporations may have access to the network of elder care programs through non-profit organizations such as the Work/Family Elder Directions, Inc., in Boston. These organizations have contracts nationwide with a network of family care managers and private and public organizations that can provide a wide range of community services for seniors. A typical scenario would be for an employee to find out that his or her mother, who lives alone on the other side of the country, has had a stroke and is hospitalized. Even after spending a month in a nursing facility, the mother is likely to return home weak and unable to care for herself. Her return home can create a broad range of difficulties, and a professional may be needed to set up a plan of care and hire the necessary services to help her handle activities of daily living. Work/Family Elder Directions, Inc., will contact a geriatric care manager with whom they have a contract. He or she will then visit the mother and develop a care plan. In this way, the employee knows that professional help has been provided and that the parent will be able to function comfortably at home.

The costs of these services may be equally important in determining their feasibility for you. Also of specific interest are the eligibility criteria for local, state, and federal government programs. For example, are there entitlements like the Meals on Wheels program, which has no income guidelines but requires a physician's approval? Or are there specific income eligibility requirements, as is the case with many of the local- and state-financed adult day care programs? Research shows that payment arrangements around the country vary significantly. For example, one rural community in northwestern Ohio levies an extra one-half of 1% of property tax to finance an extensive bus and small van service for elderly residents. One Connecticut community has a federal transportation grant coupled with municipal funds that permits an extensive Red Cross–operated transportation program for elderly, for both medical appointments and for weekly shopping trips. Such services are by no means limited to the needy, but in each case the financing is different, so it is important to explore all of these options to evaluate the "senior friendliness" of the community in question.

Another way to evaluate community services is to use The National Council on Aging, Inc.'s (NCOA) *Senior Center Standards and Self Assessment Workbook* (1990). Information on obtaining these guidelines is included in the Appendix to this book.

The sections that follow discuss in more detail the array of senior services that have been set up throughout the country. This patchwork quilt of programs ranges from one AOA-funded Area Agency on Aging that covers the entire state of New Hampshire to the non-profit Council of Senior Centers that provides extensive support to the many publicly funded senior centers in New York City. We are indebted to Ann Gillespie and Katrinka Smith Sloan's excellent book entitled *Housing Options and Services for Older Adults,* listed in the Suggested Readings at the end of this chapter, for helpful background information on several of these services.

Multi-Purpose Senior Centers

Senior centers, the most widely used community service by those over the age of 65, are designed to provide services and activities for seniors. In many communities they are or hope to become the hub of all programs and services for older persons. If not the actual provider of each service, they may serve as the coordinator for these programs and services. In this sense, a senior center is a multi-purpose organization. In 1970, there were 1,200 senior centers in the United States; by 1985, there were 10,000 senior centers, and now they number nearly 15,000.

The increase in the number of senior centers is largely the result of the Older Americans Act, which provided resources for "community facilities for the organization and provision of a

broad spectrum of services." A 1995 report estimated that more than 10 million seniors between the ages of 60 and 95 participated in the activities at over 10,000 senior centers.

Most senior centers offer information and referral services for both employment and housing and other living arrangements. Many offer health screening and will make arrangements with visiting nurse organizations and local hospital and public health offices for services as needed. Protective and legal services and information on eligibility for public benefits are also offered.

A major service provided by senior centers is meals. Many Older Americans Act–funded meal sites are located at the centers, and the centers also serve as headquarters for home-delivered meals. Community outreach services such as friendly visitor programs, home repair, and transportation are often coordinated by the senior centers.

The most common services and activities offered by senior centers are transportation to and from the center, arts and crafts, lectures, employment counseling, health screening, and day (or overnight) trips. The range and extent of the services at your local senior center depend on the level of community support and the resources of the center.

Senior centers provide many services such as communal meals, exercise programs, transportation, and health screenings.

Important factors to remember are that senior centers are designed to serve community needs. Participation is voluntary, and one can take part in selected activities intermittently or on a regular basis. In evaluating your community, therefore, it is important to take a careful look at the local senior center and speak with the staff members and seniors who participate in its activities to determine its ability to meet your needs.

Adult Day Care

The number of adult day care centers nationwide has increased from 300 in the late 1970s to an estimated 3,000 in 1994 with projections that 10,000 centers will be in operation by the year 2000.

Adult day care centers provide supervision in a group setting for older or disabled people who live at home. These centers offer many benefits, both for the family of the participant as well as for the individuals who attend. For the caregiver these centers provide respite care, and many employers consider this an important benefit permitting employees to remain more fully active at work. For the participants, the adult day care activities provide socialization and a change of scenery.

A wide range of services are offered in adult day care centers. These include:

- Skilled nursing services

- Healthcare monitoring

- Physical, occupational, and speech therapy

- Personal care

- Nutritional services

- Counseling

- Transportation

- Recreational programs

- Professional care need assessments

Shared activities add to the feeling of community in a day care center.

Adult day care standards and guidelines differ in each community. It is important to visit the center for an evaluation. A 1990 NCOA report makes the following suggestions about what to look for in an adult day care center:

- Written policies on fees and emergency procedures

- Written up-to-date plans of care for each participant

- Planned menus and meals for special diets

- Daily, planned communications with caregivers

- Referrals provided for other services

- Active, involved staff trained in cardiopulmonary resuscitation (CPR) and first aid

- Warm, inviting atmosphere

- Adequate space, furniture, and specialized equipment if specialized care is required

- A variety of social activities

The organization of adult day care can be divided into a healthcare model and a social service model. In the healthcare model, health and rehabilitation services are emphasized, and they are usually sponsored by a nursing facility or hospital. The social service model emphasizes recreation and assistance with daily activities, such as grooming, walking, and nutritional counseling. This model is usually located in a senior center, and the staff tend to be social workers and aides. There are a limited number of adult day care centers (about 5%) that only serve adults with various dementias including Alzheimer's disease. In these environments, staff has a higher level of healthcare training, and the staff-to-client ratio is higher.

Research has shown that cases of depression in the elderly have been considerably reduced by adult day care activity several days a week. A recent study conducted in California shows that adult day care delays nursing facility placement by an average of 15 to 22 months. Costs range from $20 to $50 per day, depending on the location and range of services. Adult day care costs are less than one-third to one-half the cost of nursing home care and can serve nearly anyone who is not bedridden. Medicare does not consider day care a separate reimbursable service, but specific services such as physical therapy and social and psychological services received in these settings can be reimbursed. Also, some states reimburse adult day care in their programs for low-income persons.

A recent study conducted in California shows that adult day care delays nursing facility placement by an average of 15 to 22 months.

Lifetime Learning Opportunities

Organizations often associated with the national Elderhostel movement provide a variety of continuing education courses for seniors. Other programs are offered by the Shepherd's Centers of America with over 80 locations throughout the country. A multitude of local programs also abound, such as one in which a group of retirees developed an adult learning center associated with a community college. The learning center, led by retired seniors with an active group of participants, offered a variety of educational programs for both the fall and spring terms and served 152 seniors in the first year. Courses ranged from travel seminars to courses in opera and symphony appreciation taught by local professional music teachers. Of special appeal in this kind of a program is a curriculum developed by the participants so that the courses are usually filled, and there is a great deal of interaction among the students and the teachers.

Local libraries often conduct excellent lifetime learning programs. The National Council on Aging has developed extensive program materials for study groups through its humanities program funded by the National Endowment for the Humanities, and sessions are held throughout the country.

Emphasizing the same goals is the national Elderhostel movement through which individuals can take summer courses throughout the United States and many parts of the world. These courses are inexpensive, because the participants live in college dormitories and have their meal service in the dining rooms. This movement has increased dramatically from 15 participants and five college campuses to 20,000 participants at over 300 institutions worldwide in just 19 years.

Additionally, most community and state colleges have special tuition waivers for individuals over the age of 60 or 62 enabling attendees to take just one or a full schedule of courses. Programs to obtain a high school equivalency diploma are also offered. Many states have programs such as the University Without Walls which lets you consolidate various courses into degree-granting programs. The Appendix to this book lists sources that can be contacted for more information on lifetime learning programs in your own community or around the nation.

Volunteer Programs

Among the most popular of these is the Retired Senior Volunteer Program (RSVP), a federally supported volunteer program. Many of the activities supported by these programs are intergenerational. One of the most popular is a mentoring program in which senior volunteers work as teachers' assistants in the elementary and middle schools in the community. The close relationships that often develop between the older volunteers and the children they mentor can be mutually beneficial and satisfying. Other communities under the auspices of RSVP have a time-sharing program in which an individual accumulates hours, either as a friendly visitor or by providing errand services for a homebound couple. If and when services are needed, he or she has first access to it through the Time Bank program. Other volunteer programs sponsored by RSVPs range from literacy volunteers, whereby older people work to help others learn to read and write English, to caregiver support programs such as friendly visitor and telephone reassurance programs.

Many community volunteer activities span the generations.

Another valuable intergenerational program developed by the NCOA is the Family Friends Program which links seniors with children who have chronic disabilities, homeless children, or rural families in distress. Funded originally by the Robert Wood Johnson Foundation and supported by the Administration on Aging, this is now a nationwide program in 25 locations, matching the talents of committed seniors with a variety of at-risk children and families.

Most communities have many other volunteer opportunities for seniors, and they can usually be located by contacting the local United Way and/or the local senior center.

Meals on Wheels and Nutrition Services

A major problem facing many homebound elderly is proper nutrition. Shopping for food may be difficult and cooking may no longer be interesting, especially if a person is living alone. Under the Older Americans Act, the federal government developed a national program that provides nutritionally balanced meals 5 days a week at a variety of sites in each community. Often transportation services are provided to the meal site, which gives a homebound person an opportunity to socialize.

Meals are also provided to individuals in their own homes. In fact, the Meals on Wheels program now provides almost 50% of all meals served to seniors in their own homes. Either volunteers or paid staff from the sponsoring organization will deliver two meals a day, often a hot one at noon and then a cold one for the evening, to individuals whose circumstances prevent them from preparing their own meals.

Some important factors to note about meal programs or nutrition services:

- Programs are designed for those who need them; not being able to afford to pay should not prohibit anyone from participating

- Eligibility requirements vary

- The socialization aspect may be considered more important than the meal itself by participants

Congregate meal sites give elders an opportunity to socialize.

Costs range from low to no-cost. Much of the food is donated, and the program is usually supported by local, state, or federal funds. Volunteers, who may be fellow participants, provide much of the labor. Contributions are requested, and sometimes fees are charged on a sliding scale from 50¢ to $3 a meal. This permits the sponsoring agency to increase the number of meals served.

Errand and Chore Services

These services are often organized by non-profit organizations. Volunteers run errands for homebound individuals. All volunteers are screened by the sponsoring organization and then work directly with homebound persons, either taking them to do their errands or doing the errands for them. Errand and chore services have permitted many individuals to remain in their own homes despite not being able to drive or lift and carry groceries. Because these are volunteer programs, the cost is nominal. An additional potential benefit is the opportunity for a strong personal relationship to develop between the person providing the errand service and the homebound individual.

Chore and errand programs are a vital part of assisting homebound seniors in their efforts to remain in their own homes. Such varied needs as lawn mowing, snow shoveling, leaf raking, gutter cleaning, and other minor household chores are performed by responsible individuals at a fair price.

Home Repair Programs

The Andrus Gerontology Center at the University of Southern California has developed a catalogue of many home modification programs. This is how it works: a local social service agency will learn of an individual or a couple who need to have grab bars installed or other modest modifications made to permit them to remain in their own home. Volunteers with carpentry and home modification experience will then be sent to the person's home, and the installation will be made at a very modest cost. This does not include major projects such as ramps or stairways, but volunteers can install durable medical equipment that will permit the individual to remain at home.

Senior Transportation Programs

Many communities have transportation programs for seniors. Because these programs vary throughout the country, seniors evaluating their own community or one to which they would like to move should determine the extent of these services. This is especially pertinent if the individual does not have the personal resources to hire a taxi or driver service.

Errand and chore programs enable home-bound seniors to remain in their own homes.

Escort Services

Such services arrange for people to provide transportation and also to accompany an older person to medical appointments or shopping. Both volunteers and paid escorts are used, and the programs have a variety of funding sources. Sometimes escorts assist in obtaining public transportation; at other times they use their own car or an agency vehicle.

Geriatric Medical Services and Care Management

As the elderly population continues to grow in number, the need for resources for medical advice will continue to increase as well. Often family physicians or specialists have not had significant training in geriatric medicine, and it can be difficult to locate a board-certified geriatric physician. The need for more geriatric specialists is emphasized by increasing life expectancies. Access to a major hospital and adequate home nursing and case management services can also be important for older adults.

One of the new directions in healthcare is care management whereby the responsibility for locating, coordinating, and monitoring a network of services is assumed by an individual or institution. Many large corporations offer their employees and retirees a nationwide information and referral service program that helps match services to individual needs. Included are screening and assessment, development of a plan of care, authorizing and arranging for the delivery of the service, and monitoring and reassessing needs. Whether such a service is available in a community is an important criterion for evaluating the community's elder sensitivity.

Another promising development is portable medical service. Many elderly living in their own homes receive medical services from a van with a range of newer products and services that in the past could only be obtained from hospitals or physician office visits. Consider the recent development of portable oxygen, which has permitted hundreds of individuals to walk around their homes and even travel in a car while benefitting from a continuous supply of supplemental oxygen.

Telephone Reassurance and Friendly Visiting

These are some of the oldest social service programs for seniors and are usually part of a formal community network sponsored by volunteer and public-funded agencies. They are coordinated by professional staff who recruit and supervise a group of volunteers. Calls by phone provide friendly contact and also serve such functions as reminding an individual to take medications or providing an opportunity for a quick assessment of an individual's state of mind. If contact is not made by telephone, a personal visit is made to the home.

A friendly visit can lift the spirits of a homebound individual.

Such programs are most helpful for people living alone, and they are generally targeted to more frail or vulnerable older persons. They have modest operating costs because of the large number of volunteers. There may be eligibility requirements such as living alone or being housebound, but there is no cost to the consumer.

Personal Emergency Response System

The possibility of not being able to call for assistance in case of an emergency is a major concern for older people who live alone as well as for their families. This concern can be alleviated through the purchase of a personal emergency response system of which there are currently 15 to 20 different options on the market.

This personal emergency response system has a flashing light to direct emergency personnel to the house.

A personal emergency response system is a two-way communication system that links the user to a central console by activating a button on a small transmitter. Some systems contact a central office that dispatches help. Others dial 911 directly. Many states have a 911 system whereby individuals with chronic illnesses such as a heart condition can have information programmed into the console so that when a call is received from the individual's number, personal information appears on the screen. This obviously can improve response times by emergency personnel. Some systems also have a flashing light in the window of the house that helps direct emergency personnel to the apartment or house.

Costs vary from $200 to $1,000 initially with monthly monitoring fees of $10 to $15. It is also possible to rent the unit and monitoring system for a fee of approximately $50 per month. Some costs may be reimbursable by medical insurance.

The AARP has published a booklet entitled *Product Report: PERS,* which can be ordered directly from AARP Fulfillment as referenced in the Appendix at the end of this book.

Coordination of Senior Services Programs

Many communities have a range of services for seniors, but they may be operated by non-profit organizations as well as by area agencies on aging, senior centers, and church-related groups. Some states have statewide groups that will work with an individual or his or her family to coordinate senior services for both medical and non-medical needs. It is important, however, to determine which group does this and the quality of their work. Consider the following example.

Mr. and Mrs. Jones were in their 80s and still living in their own home, able to drive, do their own shopping, and handle home maintenance. When Mrs. Jones had a stroke, however, she was hospitalized, went to a nursing home briefly, and then came back into her own home. The local Visiting Nurse Association had a social worker on the staff who put together a program of services. Unfortunately, the community did not have a home-delivered meal service, which meant that Mr. Jones had to prepare all the meals for the couple. In addition, even though there were physical therapy services that could be provided at home for Mrs. Jones, the community did not have an adult day care center. As a result, Mr. Jones became increasingly frustrated because of the amount of care he had to provide to his wife without any respite. When the burden became too much, Mrs. Jones was unable to continue to live at home. Another community with a better coordination of services might have made it possible for Mrs. Jones to remain at home much longer.

Although many other aspects of a community will factor into your evaluation of where to spend your later years, the quality, cost, and types of senior services should be given careful consideration. Fortunately, these services are widespread in larger cities and most suburbs, but if one is evaluating communities in rural areas, some services may be more difficult to access. When you combine an evaluation of such community and senior services with your family financial analysis, you will have a much better basis for making realistic decisions. The outcome of these decisions—either modifying your present home, building a new house, or moving into a retirement community—will be discussed in detail in the next three chapters.

References

American Association of Retired Persons. *Understanding Senior Housing for the 1990s.* Washington D.C.: AARP, 1990, p.8.

Boyer, Richard, and David Savageau. *Places Rated Almanac: Your Guide to Finding the Best Places to Live in America.* Chicago/New York/San Francisco: Rand McNally, 1985.

Kodner, Dennis. A Vision of Long Term Care. *Health Progress Magazine* December 1989, p.57.

National Council on Aging. *Senior Center Standards and Self Assessment Workbook,* 1990.

Peterson, Esther. *Choice Time: Thinking Ahead on Long Term Care.* Hartford, Conn.: Aetna Life Insurance and Annuity Company, 1988.

Polniaszek, Susan. *Insurance to Pay for Long-Term Care.* Washington, D.C.: United Seniors Health Cooperative, April, 1992.

U.S. Bureau of the Census. *1990 Census of Population and Housing, Nursing Home Population, 1990.* CPH-L-137. Washington, D.C.: U.S. Government Printing Office, 1990.

Suggested Readings

Gillespie, Ann E., and Katrinka Smith Sloan, *Housing Options and Services for Older Adults.* Santa Barbara, Calif.: ABC-CLIO, Inc., 1990.

Golant, Stephen M. *Housing America's Elderly: Many Possibilities/Few Choices.* Newbury Park, Calif.: Sage Publications, 1992.

Pynoos, Jon, and others. *Linkages: Long Term Care Digest.* Los Angeles, Calif.: Long Term Care National Resource Center at USC, 1990.

Scholen, K. *Home-made Money: Consumer's Guide to Home Equity Conversion.* Washington, D.C.: AARP, 1991.

Chapter Four

Modifying Your Present House

Perhaps in our later years, when we are no longer so completely defined by those roles of family and professional career that structured our youth, *home*—the place from which we come and go, the place with which we are intimately familiar, whose very furnishings express the roots and order of our being—is more important to our essential sense of selfhood and well-being than any gerontological care. Whatever its gerontological shortcomings, mysteriously one's own home "maximizes a sense of personal competence," the gerontologists themselves admit. It can even sustain "the ability to maintain independence despite failing physiological and sensory capabilities ..."

(Betty Friedan, *The Fountain of Age*, p. 350)

Getting Help

We will assume in this chapter that you have now analyzed the "elder" sensitivity of your community and completed your personal assessments, including a careful consideration of your desire to be near friends and family. You have evaluated your finances, shopped your various options, and have now decided that modifying your present home is the best solution for you. Because these are all such difficult issues I want to introduce the process of modifying your own home with some additional background to help you feel comfortable with this decision, as well as help you plan and implement the best possible, personal home modifications.

A recent housing study by the Russell Sage Foundation, a major national research organization, found that older people living in their own single family house or apartment are in environments similar in basic design to those occupied by younger persons. This is true even in cases where individuals may have one or more chronic health conditions that restrict their activities. A survey conducted by the American Association of Retired Persons (AARP) found that 86% of those over the age of 55 want to remain in their own homes. While some have moved to retirement communities to better accommodate their needs, the majority of seniors have decided to "age in place." Housing modifications will probably be needed to help you accomplish your goal, and getting professional advice will be important in planning and executing the work based on your needs, abilities, resources, and limitations.

One Chicago company specializes in meeting the needs for both older clients and younger people with disabilities. It utilizes the expertise of professionals including occupational therapists, architects, and home remodelers to identify needs and help develop and implement plans for home modification. The company will work with you to:

- Determine your specific needs through a free in-hospital and/or in-home assessment.

- Recommend and review a list of specific modifications to your home that will meet your needs.

- Develop with you an ideal home modification program and estimate the costs consistent with your budget.

- Implement the plan and consult periodically with you to adapt your home to meet your changing lifestyle needs.

In addition to major home modifications, this company offers a full range of products including ramps, stair lifts, wheelchair lifts, grab bars, roll-in showers, modified door openings, and accessibility and safety products for the home.

An organization that can help you locate such a company in your own area is The National Policy and Resource Center for Housing and Support Services located at the University of Southern California in Los Angeles. It has an extensive database on home modification programs throughout the United States. For more information, write the Center at the University of Southern California, Andrus Gerontology Center, Los Angeles, CA 90089-0191.

The National Association of Homebuilders and Remodelers in Washington, DC (800/368-5242) also offers programs and information on accessibility modifications and products, as does the Center for Universal Design in Raleigh, North Carolina (800/220-8770).

Goals of Modification

In order to make sensible decisions about what your efforts should accomplish, considerable research should be undertaken. For example, do you want an arrangement in which you can live entirely on the ground floor, thus eliminating the use of stairs? Are your present bathrooms, kitchen, and living areas comfortable and easy to use?

Other issues should be considered as well. Do you want a caregiver apartment or a separate living area for visiting family and friends? Should you become partially immobilized and require a caregiver, a "user-friendly" house with a caregiver apartment can become a helpful recruiting factor. Many communities do allow caregiver apartments for older couples, and it is important that this issue be examined through the local planning and zoning boards. It is interesting to note that in Europe single-family homes are the exception rather than the rule.

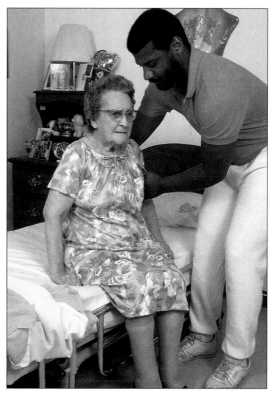

A caregiver apartment within your home can ease the caregiver's challenges.

Finally, in your goals for home modification, it is most helpful to try to anticipate the kinds of changes required. For example, if your family history indicates a potential for mobility problems, it would be wise to involve a professional team in your planning.

Steps in Planning

Once you determine your goals for modification, the next step is to hire an architect or home remodeler who is knowledgeable about accessibility issues and familiar with the vast array of "age-friendly" products on the market. Qualifications to look for include knowledge of potential zoning problems and fire codes—for example, proper access to a second floor of the home if a caregiver apartment with separate entrance is being considered. This individual should also be able to help determine an appropriate size for any additions as well as how to accomplish specific modifications for improved accessibility of the kitchen and bath.

One problem many people have encountered is the lack of cosmetic appeal afforded by many products on the market. Some people will install institutional-type grab bars in the bathroom, giving the room a hospital appearance. On the other hand, using brightly colored grab bars that blend in with the rest of the decor can make a tremendous difference in how "user-friendly" a home is and how well it works visually.

An architect can suggest products and modifications to meet your specific needs.

The planning homeowners do can also be done by those who rent homes or apartments. Obviously, you will first have to consult with your landlord, but according to the Americans With Disabilities Act, an individual can modify a rental unit for accessibility provided he or she agrees to return the unit to its earlier condition when vacating the premises.

Non-Structural Modifications

Although structural home modifications or additions are a major cost concern, simple changes like rearranging furniture, eliminating trailing wires on the floor, clearing passageways of excess or oversized furniture, and other relatively simple alterations can make a home much more user-friendly without remodeling. *The Perfect Fit: Creative Ideas for a Safe and Livable Home* published by AARP offers a simple checklist to help you identify non-structural modifications.

Accessibility Issues and Modifications

Site and Entrance
Because of a variety of factors including the slope of the land, type of house (split-level, one-story, or two-story), and construction methods (frame or slab), modifying a house for accessibility often becomes more difficult and costly than building a new

A ramp with railings on both sides makes this house accessible for individuals with impaired mobility.

house. The major accessibility issue in an existing home is how to eliminate steps at the entrance to reach living spaces as well as steps along routes to the garden, the garage, and other areas of the property.

One-story houses are the easiest structures to modify because all living spaces are already on one floor. Split-level houses are probably the most difficult to modify. In these structures, the levels are staggered at half levels, and rooms required for daily living like the kitchen, bathrooms, and bedrooms may all be on different floors. Stair spaces are usually too small for lifts or elevators, and entrances often require one to go up or down to reach living spaces.

Two-story houses usually have smaller ground areas than split-level or ranch-style homes, and attention should be given to establishing complete living facilities on the ground floor. Second floors can only be made fully accessible with stair lifts or home elevators.

Accessible entrances can be built in a variety of ways and can often eliminate hard-to-reach steps and slopes that would make it impossible to modify the house. Options include:

- Relocating the entrance to an area where access is easier

- Regrading to permit a gently sloping walk to the entrance

- Constructing earth berms with bridges to reach the ground floor

Landscaping can often make these modifications attractive while permitting easy access.

Gardens

In evaluating your home site for potential modifications, it is important to evaluate the yard and property to see how the garden, yard, and lawn can meet your goals and how you can simplify their care. Other books are specifically devoted to this subject, but the following checklist will identify the major considerations:

1. Make sure the garden and yard can be viewed from indoors and have access to water and electric power sources.

2. Consider starting small then expanding the size of the garden or yard based on your interests.

3. Recognize the need for shaded areas to work in while maintaining a sunny section for growing.

4. A level site is best, but if working with sloping areas, consider attractive ramping and non-slip, non-reflective paving materials for passageways. Avoid sudden and unexpected changes in direction of pathways and include plenty of handrails at appropriate intervals.

5. Make sure water supply is easy to access and use. Consider various types of wall-mounted hose reels and trickle hoses for areas requiring additional watering.

Gardening can be very rewarding.

6. Consider building raised beds as well as using plants that are easy to reach either when sitting down or with long-handled tools from a standing position. Determine your most comfortable gardening position and place plants so that they can be reached easily from this position.

7. Try to plant a garden that is full of sensory stimuli all year long.

8. Lawns are hard work to maintain; make sure you have the best tools available to maintain your lawn and consider replacing excessive lawn with lower maintenance ground cover.

9. Plan a garden that can be modified, if necessary, to help prevent wandering by an individual who has dementia or episodes of confusion.

Reaching the House from the Car

Depending on your primary mode of transportation, you may have to plan for transfers from the bus stop or garage. Options include a convenient drop-off point in the case of a detached garage or creating a direct entrance into the house from an attached garage. There are as many solutions to this problem as there are variations of the problem, and it may be helpful to note just one. In the case of a house that sits on a hill above the street, it may be possible to open an area behind the house so that a car can be driven up to a wooden deck in back with a gradual ramp to the rear door. The key is to improve accessibility into the house and then identify modifications that are most cost effective and easy to use.

Approach to the Home

A gradual slope eliminates the need for stairs.

Sloping walks make excellent approaches because they may eliminate the need for handrails. A shallow slope is ideal and probably should not exceed 1 inch of elevation for every 20 inches in length. Another way to handle an approach on some sloping sites is to use a bridge from the entrance to the ground on the uphill side of the house. Benches and planters along level stretches of bridging can create an attractive alternative to handrails. Shallow ramps combined with walks and decks can be landscaped attractively and provide easy-to-use entrances in contrast to the often unattractive standard ramp with handrails. Private houses do not have to meet federal accessibility guidelines, but these should be kept in mind to be sure that the solution is safe for you. By using an architect you can usually determine the most attractive and the safest solution for access to either the front or rear entrance of the house.

Entrances

Several features can be incorporated into home entrances to ensure safety and accessibility. An entrance generally consists of the actual door, the floor or ground area on either side of the door, the adjacent structure of the building, and the route usually used to enter.

The essential features of an entrance and the design around it should include:

- Level and clear floor space both inside and outside with a slight slope for water run-off on the outside

- A flush or low threshold

A ramp from the garage to the home's interior improves accessibility and does not affect the appearance of the home's exterior.

- At least a 36-inch wide door

- Door, including storm doors, that open with a light amount of force

- Easily operated lock and levered handle

- Covering above entrance to protect against inclement weather

- A shelf for packages or other materials being brought into or taken out of the house

- Peepholes or viewing windows in or on the side of the door

- Proper lighting, especially around the lock

- Power door opener for narrow doors with strong springs

Screen and Storm Doors

Screen and storm doors can sometimes be difficult for an older person. Standard aluminum screen/storm doors are generally mounted with a strong pump, which

This entrance door features a levered handle and a side window for viewing outdoors.

makes them difficult to open and then slide the catch to keep them open when entering with packages or boxes. In most cases it is probably best to remove the pump entirely and just leave the chain to be sure the door will not fly open. Another option is to remove the door if it continues to cause difficulties.

Maneuvering Space

The maneuvering space around doors can cause problems for older people. Most existing housing has been built with corridors and doorways that are too narrow to meet current standards. Solutions to increase access are discussed in the following sections.

Door Swings and Widths

Major door accessibility problems are width and door swing. With a requirement of 32 to 36 inches clear width for easy passage with crutches or wheelchair, most doors in the United States are inadequate. As a result, most accessibility modifications must consider replacing doors as well as the frames around them, two improvements that can be quite expensive.

Other accessibility features are adequate floor space in front of doors on either side to allow opening and closing the door as well as on the side where the door handle or latch is located. The threshold should be flush with the floor surface for easier passage, and the door handle should be workable with a clenched fist, especially for individuals with arthritis. The door should be responsive to a minimum of force.

The usable space in a doorway is less than its outside dimensions because of moldings and door clearance.

Another important consideration regarding door width is the "clear width," or the opening space for passage. When a door is open, the width of the door reduces the passage area. An easy way to test your door widths for accessibility is to borrow a wheelchair or a walker and try to get through the various doors in your home. Accessibility problems will become quite obvious after a few attempts to move through standard doors.

The size of your home's hallways may also present accessibility problems. With a wheelchair or walker, try to determine not only how hard it may be to move through a hallway, but also to see if it is even possible to turn easily from a hallway into a doorway. Most guidelines specify at least a 3-foot 6-inch hallway, although a 4-foot hallway would be ideal. Many newer homes have bi-fold doors that often come off their track. Additionally, when they are opened, the fold reduces the hallway space by at least 6 inches. A new opening and closing device by the Kiwi Connection has just been patented. It supports the door better at the top and also allows the bi-fold doors to be opened flat against the side of the corridor.

Types of Doors

Door types include hinge, sliding, pocket, bi-fold, and folding. Certain features of each door type can either make the door easier or more difficult for use by individuals with restricted mobility.

The most common type of door found in the home is a *hinge door.* These doors can be easily opened and closed when properly installed and set in the correct location between rooms. The only major drawback with the hinge door is that it requires a large amount of clear floor space. If the hinge door is narrower than 32 inches, there are several simple steps that can be taken to achieve a maximum opening space. One step is to use swing- clear door hinges, which permit a door to swing all the way open against the outer wall and adds roughly an inch of space to the opening. Another way is to remove the trim on both sides of the door, which can provide another inch of space.

Sliding doors can provide easy access, especially to closets. If each side can provide a 32-inch minimum clearance with loop-shaped handles on the outside of each door, these doors can be easy to manipulate.

Pocket doors are recommended to avoid problems caused by a door's swing. These doors require less floor space, but they may have some disadvantages in that the standard handle and latch installed on them may be difficult to operate because they

Pocket doors increase the usable space of a doorway.

Bifold doors require less space to open. They can increase closet accessibility for those whose mobility is impaired.

are recessed into the face of the door. This can be overcome by installing loop-shaped handles, but these need to be attached to the outer edge of the door, thus reducing the clear space by at least 1 to 2 inches.

Folding doors can be difficult to operate because of their flexible construction. They are made of multiple panels attached or hinged together, and they function much like an accordion. The door frame needs to be wide enough to contain the folded door and still allow adequate passage.

A final consideration regarding doors are ways to increase the clear opening. Obviously, the simplest solution is to remove the door completely, if possible. This will increase the door width by 1 to 1 1/2 inches. A second solution is to install swing-away hinges, which allow an inch or more of doorway opening. These doors can be opened 90 degrees or more allowing the door to extend fully out of the doorway. A more expensive solution is to enlarge the doorway and replace the door and door frame. Reversing the door's swing can increase access, especially in the bathroom if the door currently swings directly into the bathroom.

Thresholds

Raised thresholds are another consideration in your planning. In most cases, a consultant will recommend that the threshold be removed completely so that there is no obstacle between rooms. If a threshold cannot be removed, it should be lowered to a 1/4-inch level change or a 1/2-inch level change with tapering on both sides. Many remodelers overlook the potential to trip on the edges of wall-to-wall carpeting, which often stops at hallways and room boundaries and is held in place by a metal border. To prevent tripping the floor should be as level and as even as possible.

Hardware

Door hardware is another important consideration. Eliminating rounded door knobs can ease maneuvering around the house for people of all ages. Levers are easy to operate for people who cannot grasp or twist; push plates on doors with latches are easy to operate; and large fixed handles without latches and/or a fixed loop make it easy for a hand to slide behind for opening and closing. Although you can purchase modified door knobs to fit over rounded knobs, this is not an attractive solution and lever-handle lock sets are now available in a variety of styles, prices and materials that are attractive and more usable. Key holes and keys can be a problem for individuals with grasping and/or visual disabilities. There are many devices on the market that will hold a key firmly and allow it to be controlled by the whole hand. Other options are push-button combination locks for individuals with little ability to twist or grasp and electronic door openers for automobiles and garage doors.

Amount of Force

The amount of force required to open a door can be a problem. A federal standard specifies that no more than 8.5 pounds of force on exterior doors and 5 pounds of force on interior doors should be required. This applies to all types of interior and exterior doors, including hinge doors, sliding doors, and pocket doors. Individuals with limited hand or arm mobility may not be able to use any type of manually operated door. Electronic door openers, controlled by a push-type wall switch or a device similar to those used for garage doors, can be installed on both exterior and interior doors. These door openers can be programmed so that only individuals with the properly coded device can open the door.

Windows

For individuals who use crutches, canes, walkers, or wheelchairs, hardware can help improve a window in several ways:

- A clear space should be available in front of each window so a person can get close enough to open, shut, and lock the window.

- Window hardware should be within a comfortable reach.

- Window should be easy to open and close with one hand.

There must be considerable clear floor space, either for a forward reach or a side reach access to the window. Window height also should be 18 to 36 inches above the floor so that a person can open or close the window from a seated position. The

Open space in front of a window is important when using a cane, walker, or wheelchair.

amount of force required to operate the window should be appropriate for the user. This is particularly important for a double-hung window, which is much more difficult to close than a crank-operated unit.

There are various types of windows, but the single- and double-hung units, which are the most common, are also the most difficult to operate. Anyone with restricted mobility will probably encounter some difficulty opening and closing single- and double-hung windows. They require strength and gripping ability, and there is a tendency for the window to stick in the track. One alternative is a device that converts the raising of the window to a crank motion, which makes it much easier to operate. Another option is to add an auxiliary handle at the bottom to help open and close the lower window.

Sliding windows are usually easier to maneuver than double-hung windows. They must, however, be properly oiled and maintained to keep the track easily movable and free of debris. Another benefit of the sliding window is that the lock is usually mounted at the bottom of the frame and within reach. An auxiliary handle can be added to the frame to make it easier to use. Casement windows are probably the easiest to operate. They are opened and closed with a crank, although at times the lock can be difficult to operate. Proper maintenance with casement windows is important.

Other types of windows include awning units and storm windows. With awning units, the window lock is part of the operating mechanism, and it is automatically engaged when the window is closed. Storm windows are used primarily on sliding and double-hung windows. They make the operation of the window significantly more complicated and often cannot be operated by anyone with restricted mobility. A possible option is to install sliding storm windows with sliding windows. The ideal option would be to replace these windows with double-paned glass and to use some of the newer operating mechanisms that come with these units.

Kitchens

As a focal point in any house, the kitchen requires careful planning and design to be safe, comfortable, and functional. As in any other major modification, close consultation with an architect and designer is important.

Designing a completely operational kitchen for someone with restricted mobility requires special attention to details and space requirements. Important considerations include the need to be able to sit down while performing certain tasks and the ability to move about with crutches, canes, walkers, or wheelchairs. The key design issues are adequate maneuvering space and reach. On the other hand, for individuals who have or anticipate visual and hearing impairments the key design issues are appropriate signals and controls.

It is important to include devices in the kitchen that will make it easier for a care-

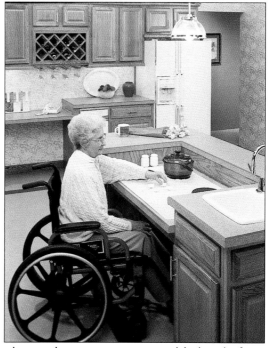

This cooktop is at an accessible height for this wheelchair-dependent homemaker.
Courtesy Whirlpool Home Appliance, Benton Harbor, Michigan

Adjustable shelves allow frequently used foods to be placed at a level convenient for this wheelchair-dependent homemaker.
Courtesy Whirlpool Home Appliance, Benton Harbor, Michigan

giver to assist an older person with vision, hearing, or mobility problems. (Chapter 5 offers specific guidelines and details in the discussion of building a new house.) The following suggestions can be incorporated in kitchen modifications.

Maneuvering Space

Although this issue primarily affects wheelchair users, it also affects people with other types of mobility problems. In most cases maneuvering space means the ability to bring a wheelchair to either a parallel or a forward approach as well as provide a sufficient turning radius. This, in effect, requires a minimum of 2 feet 6 inches by 4 feet of clear floor area and a 5-foot diameter turning space that permits a complete 360-degree turn. In addition, knee space under work surfaces should be at least 30 inches wide, 27 inches high, and 19 inches deep. The preferred size, however, is 36 inches wide because this permits an even greater turning space. In addition, it is important to note that the knee space should be unobstructed. If disposals or other plumbing materials are in the way, padding or insulation can be installed to prevent body contact with hot or sharp surfaces. Adaptability is key. It is preferable that all cabinet fronts be eas-

Maneuvering space needs to account for the turning radius of a wheelchair.

ily removed if and when a resident needs to use a wheelchair in the kitchen.

Range of Reach and Height

Individuals using either wheelchairs or sitting down while performing kitchen tasks usually can only reach forward in a range of 15 to 48 inches above the floor. This makes it impossible for the seated person to reach either conventional base or wall cabinets.

People who are standing will have slightly different limitations. They can usually reach the lower level shelves of standard wall cabinets, but they may not be able to use the lower or rear portions of the base cabinet storage. Complicating this issue is the fact that they may need to use their arms and hands to keep balance and, thus, they may have difficulty reaching and lifting objects that are too high or low. In view of these factors, a suggested reach range for such individuals is 2 to 6 feet above the floor.

Counter heights are another important kitchen modification. The standard kitchen counter is 3 feet high, but 30 to 34 inches is usually much more comfortable for a seated person. A variety of options can be considered. This can be accomplished inexpensively by installing wall brackets so that the counters can be raised or lowered, depending on the needs of the individual. For sinks, plumbing connections can be made with flexible tubing so that they can be raised and lowered without any difficulty. Other options include purchasing kitchen cabinets that can be raised or lowered by an electric motor. (Examples are shown in the kitchen for the Middletown House in Chapter 5.) The main purpose, however, is to permit the raising and lowering of the cabinets to meet the dual height needs of all users.

Other ways of meeting the needs of people with mobility problems affecting reach include the use of full-extension drawers. These drawers are deep and extend the full depth of the base cabinets. Such drawers display the contents and place them within easy reach. Rotating or sliding cabinet shelves in existing cabinets and pull-out surfaces for more work space can also be used. Rolling carts that fit into knee spaces underneath the countertops can provide additional storage space. These carts are easy to roll out when the knee space is used, and they can provide convenient work space and a safe method for transporting food from the counter to the table. Other options include countertop storage units that can be easily reached and utilize the space underneath the overhanging cabinets and at the back of the countertop.

Ranges, Cooktops, and Wall Ovens

The controls on the front panel of this oven make it easier for this wheelchair-dependent homemaker to prepare meals.
Courtesy Whirlpool Home Appliance, Benton Harbor, Michigan

The standard range has a cooking surface 35 to 36 inches above the floor. This is satisfactory for most people who are able to stand without difficulty, but not easy to work with if one is in a seated position. Therefore, it might be necessary to use a drop-front oven. The same concern applies to the controls for ranges. For short people it is very difficult to reach over hot pans to operate controls. In most cases, the controls should be mounted in the front. However this might pose a problem for families with small children. Another problem usually occurs with the standard stove that has an oven below and a range on top. The ovens are usually too low for most standing individuals with impaired mobility. One solution is to install a drop-front oven instead of a standard combination oven and range. Side-hinge doors are best for many people because they can get closer to the oven, and it requires less reaching or bending while moving hot pans.

Sinks and Refrigerators

Sinks that are going to be used by seated people should be relatively shallow with drains located as far to the rear as possible so that plumbing connections do not obstruct the knee space. Such sinks can be installed in lower countertops and adjusted to the needs of the individual. Disposals are valuable additions in the accessible kitchen, but can be a barrier for seated users. Other options include having a double sink with the disposal under the one sink and a work space next to the other sink.

For maximum accessibility, the side-by-side refrigerator is recommended and works well for most people. Ice and water dispensers on the outside can also make the unit considerably easier to use. One of the difficulties with a freezer on the top is that it cannot be reached by a seated person.

Kitchen Controls

Essentially we are concerned with levers instead of buttons, levered handles on faucets, range/oven controls that change color to indicate heat, and a variety of add-on tactile panels for visually impaired individuals. Controls that must be pushed down and then turned are difficult for many people to use. Light switches are also an important consideration, and there are three easy-to-use types: the rocker, toggle, and touch-type electronic switches, all of which can be operated by a single touch and require little force. Switches are better placed on the lower cabinet within easy reach so the user need not reach back so far. Cabinets should also be opened and closed by using loop handles rather than the many finger-gripping adaptations on the market.

Bathrooms

The bathroom is undeniably the most important room in your planning. Properly designed units including the toilet, sink, shower area, and tub make a significant difference in allowing people to remain in their homes as long as possible.

Many research projects have tried to make a 5- by 7-foot bathroom accessible, but most architects and contractors will argue that the best solution is to expand such a room by using adjoining closets, hallways, and other nearby space in order to make this important room easier to use. However, if it is clearly impossible to find the space to make a larger bathroom, it is possible to manage with a 5- by 7-foot space. The 1990 *Seniors Housing News* discussed the Groner project, a floor plan of a remodeled 5- by 7-foot bathroom. The design shown here is an example of the remodeling of a 40 to 50 year old non-expandable 5- by 7-foot bathroom. The whole bathroom had to be gutted, and the framing for the wall and the floor repaired. In this case, a rubber membrane shower liner was installed across the entire floor and part way up the walls. Walls were then reinforced with a blocking or layer of 3/4-inch plywood across the face of the studs for the installation of grab bars. In addition, the bathroom entrance was widened from 2 feet 4 inches to 3 feet.

Because the room was designed to accommodate a shower chair that rolled into the shower area, there was no need for a permanent or moveable shower bench. The standard shower head was replaced with a hand-held model. Grab bars were installed on the back and sides of the shower area for safety, and a new type of shower curtain, which folds in an accordion fashion and directs water inside rather than out, was also used. On the floor of the shower area, the rubber membrane was covered with a mortar bed to permit a pitch toward the drain and then covered with a non-skid tile. The toilet was set at 19 inches. The countertop holding the sink was carried over the top of the toilet tank creating extra storage and was hinged for tank access. The

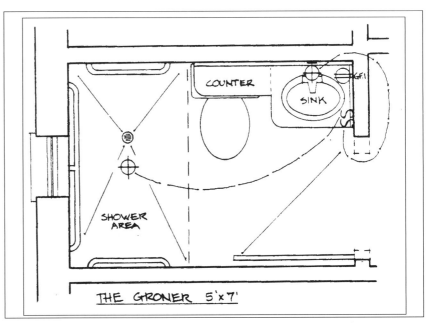

This floor plan shows a wheelchair accessible bathroom for a minimal (5' x 7') space.

overall appearance is one of a normal bath with designer fixtures and accessories. Because of the limited room, the standard tub was exchanged for a roll-in shower.

There are a variety of materials on the market, including Mipolan, to construct waterproof, non-skid floor surfaces. In addition, one can now purchase a complete 5-foot 5-inch roll-in shower, which has a slight lip so that you can roll a shower chair over it and into the unit. Other options for the shower area include a small lip or raised floor area, a sloping floor to the drain, and a folding drainage seat, which makes it easier to use the shower area. Controls must also be easily accessible from the seat, and in all cases a hand-held showerhead on a slide-bar mount works most successfully. It is also important to be able to control the water temperature, both for the tub and the shower. Thermostatically controlled valves can eliminate the problem of turning on scalding water.

On balance, roll-in showers are probably the most versatile bathing design for all ages. The space makes it easier to utilize a roll-in shower chair, and the grab bars are helpful for all people.

One of the problems with most toilets is that they are usually too low for people with disabilities. Therefore, the toilet in this bathroom should have a height of about 19 inches. This works well with transfers from wheelchairs and also helps a person with any mobility impairment to get up and down from the toilet more easily.

Grab bars should be able to support at least 250 pounds of force in any direction. Without the backing, it is usually a very expensive job because the wall has to be opened from the other side, and if the bars are to be installed in the shower or tub area, one must drill through tiles. Therefore, the ideal solution is to install the plywood backing so that the grab bars can be attached securely without damaging the tiles. Grab bars should be exactly 1 1/2 inches away from the wall. A wider gap can cause a user's arm to slip through the space between the wall and the bar. A smaller gap does not allow enough space for the user's hands and knuckles. Grab bars are now available in a variety of shapes, colors, and materials so that the bathroom does not look institutional.

This toilet seat is 19 inches from the floor, a height convenient for most individuals with disabilities.
Courtesy Hewi, Inc., Lanaster, Pennsylvania

These grab bars decrease the risk of falling in the bathroom.
Courtesy Hewi, Inc., Lanaster, Pennsylvania

Lighting, Soundproofing, Safety Alarm, and Communication Systems

Lighting is probably one of the most important features in home modification. One must consider both night lighting (including task lighting) and daytime lighting. Glare can be a severe daytime problem, especially for individuals with impaired vision. One solution is to install skylights, especially over the bathroom if this is possible, and various window treatments such as blinds to reduce glare.

Soundproofing is also important. Soundproofing can make the house quieter, especially if a section of the house is on the ground floor and below the apartment of the caregiver. In one home modification project, two-by-fours were laid over a soundproofing material placed on the studs, and a new floor was floated on the two-by-fours.

There are a variety of security systems that can be included in the house. Sometimes these modifications are expensive in an older home, but wireless alarm systems are now available so that walls need not be opened to install new wiring. In addition, there are numerous electronic devices that will activate various appliances by the click of a hand-held device. A security system and fire alarm connected directly to an alarm company is ideal. Many companies will provide a free estimate and will work closely with the architect and/or contractor to install the proper system.

The Caregiver Apartment

A major decision to be made early in a home modification program is whether a caregiver apartment can or should be built into the home. If the house is all on one floor, this might be done by either utilizing the basement if it is accessible or adding additional square footage to the home. A prefabricated accessory apartment is another option and can be installed directly into your one- or two-car garage. With a two-story house, it is probably less expensive to modify the ground floor for accessibility and assume that the caregiver apartment would be on the second floor. Zoning must be carefully researched. Each case will be different so it is important that the family review this carefully with the architect to decide what would be the most cost-effective way to modify the house and at the same time provide comfortable living accommodations for the residents as they get older.

The stairways also require your attention in home modification. In some cases it might be less expensive to install an ele-

A caregiver apartment is provided on the second floor of this house.

vator or possibly an electric stair glide. A recent example was a very large four-bedroom colonial-style home converted into a two-family house by installing an elevator in the corner of the dining room. Because it was a large home, this was done quite unobtrusively with the younger family members living on the ground floor, and the older members of the family using the separate apartment on the second floor.

Supervising the Work

Although the emphasis in this book is on the planning process, it is important to anticipate some of the more practical steps you can take to facilitate the remodeling process.

Once the plans are completed, the next step is to hire a contractor or act as your own contractor. If you need to hire a contractor, you should search for contractors who have a reputation for good business practices. If you have hired an architect to do the planning for you, the architect can help you locate a responsible contractor and also supervise the estimating process and work completion. This assures continuity and is well worth the expense if you do not have the time or expertise to deal with the project on a day-to-day basis. Usually the architect gives a set of plans and specifications to several contractors in whom he has confidence. Each contractor will then price the plans and specifications and submit contracts for the complete job. In most cases there will be differences in each estimate, and the architect will make recommendations to you. Once you have selected the contractor, the architect will then supervise the job to make sure that the project is being done according to the plans and specifications. This can be an extremely valuable service and helps avoid pitfalls such as inferior materials or sloppy workmanship. Architects will approve various stages of the project so that you can make partial payments as the work is completed. A certain portion of the funds may be reserved to ensure that any unfinished work is completed before final payment is made.

A less-expensive approach is to find the contractor yourself. If so, you will want to ask for a list of other customers, talk with them, and even visit their homes to ascertain the quality of the contractor's work. Also check other sources such as local banks, state contractor licensing boards, business groups like the Chamber of Commerce, the local Association of Home Builders or Remodelers, and other contractors. Once you have selected one or more candidates, use the same process an architect would and submit the plans and specifications for estimates. It is important to obtain at least three estimates and then evaluate them to determine who should be given the job. There are many factors to consider before you sign the contract, and it is wise to have a lawyer or someone familiar with contracts assist you in the evaluation. Issues that should be covered include a clear description of the work, including material specifications, payment schedules, permits and licenses, contractor liabilities such as responsibility for workmen's compensation and other liability insurance, and unconditional lien releases from subcontractors. Once the job is underway, you will have to supervise it and make payments as work is completed to your satisfaction.

As we indicated earlier, an important matter to consider before you begin any large-scale project is local zoning. This is important if you are building a caregiver or accessory apartment addition or modification. Communities of single-family homes continue to be a problem, and it may be necessary to obtain a variance, which can be time consuming and aggravating. Often this is the reason for hiring an architect to work with you in the planning phase of the project, because he or she will be aware of local zoning regulations and can assist you in obtaining the necessary approvals.

We strongly advise you to avoid contractors who solicit door-to-door for this type of work, to know what you are signing (especially with contracts), and to keep a complete file of the project.

Should you decide to act as your own contractor, be aware of the risks. Even though you may do this to save money, inexperience can cost money; it takes more time, financing may be more difficult to obtain, and your life is bound to be disrupted. If you decide to go ahead on your own, here is a checklist to help you avoid common pitfalls:

1. Plan ahead and do as much research as possible such as pricing and shopping for materials.

2. Check with the lender to be sure you can get your loan for the project.

3. Check the subcontractor's references.

4. Have a good set of plans and specifications to which you can hold subcontractors accountable.

5. Obtain necessary permits.

6. Create a job schedule.

7. Check your insurance risks.

8. Supervise the job carefully and anticipate disruptions to your normal life.

9. Schedule payments to coincide with the work schedule and only make them after work has been inspected and approved by you and your local building inspector.

10. Check subcontractors' suppliers. You still need to be protected from a mechanic's lien in case your subcontractor has not paid the suppliers.

Modifications to Accommodate Common Age-Related Changes and Conditions

CONSIDERATIONS	SUGGESTED MODIFICATIONS

Vision

■ *Pupils get smaller and less light enters the eye. Cornea of eye yellows, decreasing depth perception and making it difficult to tolerate glare.*

| Are floor level changes easily observed? | Install brighter bulbs; replace incandescent with fluorescent or halogen lights. Fix broken or uneven sidewalks and paths. Mark stairs that have high gloss finishes with tape or paint edge white. Rearrange rugs and furniture and eliminate loose phone wires and other obstructions. |
| Is illumination adjusted throughout house? | Light evenly. Avoid two side-by-side bright colors. Avoid using shiny surfaces to help minimize glare. |

■ *Eyes adjust to dark much more slowly. At 30 years, the eye takes 2-3 minutes to adjust to dark. At 80, it takes over 10 minutes.*

| Can the individual see well enough to turn on switches, walk safely in the house, and open and unlock doors? | Install illuminated lights in apartments, corridors, cellar stairs. Install brighter fluorescent tubes, especially near door to facilitate using the key. Provide key extender to ease opening. |

■ *Spots or "floaters" are common; conditions such as glaucoma, cataracts, diabetic retinopathy, and macular degeneration cause visual difficulties for many older adults.*

| Can the individual use telephones and read instructions, and are alarm systems usable? Can controls on stoves and other devices be seen and used? | Obtain assistive devices such as illuminated magnifiers, reading stands, and other products that can be helpful to individuals with impaired vision. Install large-button telephones and sound alarms in all areas of the home (i.e., to be accessible when sleeping, cooking, recreating, bathing, etc.). Consider large TV and computer screens. |

Hearing

■ *Presbycusis, which affects most older adults, makes it difficult to hear high-pitched sounds such as women's voices and consonants.*

| Are floors carpeted and curtains in windows to reduce sharp noises and distracting echoes? | Inspect all rooms and recommend carpeting and wall and window coverings. Also if a person cannot hear the phone or alarm, AT&T has a device that converts the phone or alarm ring to a flashing light. |
| Have you considered special electronic devices such as vibrating beds and alarm clocks, amplified TV sets and telephones? | Prepare a list of special-needs products from your local telephone company and AT&T as well as kitchen aids such as colored stove controls and announcing information and flashing lights and warnings. |

Modifications to Accommodate Common Age-Related Changes and Conditions *(continued)*

CONSIDERATIONS	SUGGESTED MODIFICATIONS

■ *Background noises can compound hearing difficulties.*

Are sleeping and conversation areas near major appliances?	Inspect noisy units such as dishwashers and washing machines to be sure they are properly installed. It may be necessary to replace them with quieter, newer units. Also explore proper insulation between floors and noisy rooms.

Mobility and Dexterity
■ *Arthritis is the major cause of mobility problems.*

Do the controls in the home comply with the "rule of thumb" by which an able-bodied person can operate a control with the fist?	Replace all doorknobs with levers that can be opened with a closed fist, the simplest and least expensive solution. Modify the home of individuals with arthritis in the knees and hips with sinks that move up and down and toilets that are at least 19 inches from the floor.

■ *Other forms of arthritis, including the type in which the body's joints experience degenerative changes, impose further limitations on mobility.*

Have you considered how accessible various areas of the home are to someone seated in a wheelchair or standing with the aid of a walker or crutches?	Adjust tension needed to open and close doors. Move the bedroom and bathroom to the ground floor if the individual cannot maneuver the stairs. Modify cabinet height and toilet facilities.

Frailty and Disease-Related Limitations
■ *Chronic conditions such as heart disease, stroke, hardening of arteries, and osteoporosis may necessitate particular modifications.*

Are you using furnishings that are stable without sharp corners to minimize the effect of falls?	Make environment safe by removing scatter rugs, objects and clutter, but keep layout of familiar furniture and pathways the same. Consider placing barriers at dangerous locations to prevent unstable or disoriented individuals from falling down stairs or entering unfamiliar rooms.
Are you aware that walking from one place to another can be extremely difficult for people with limited mobility and particularly dangerous for those with heart disorders?	Consider relocating bedrooms or living spaces to the same level, establishing convenient open storage areas, and removing hazards on paths between commonly used rooms.

Modifications to Accommodate Common Age-Related Changes and Conditions
(continued)

CONSIDERATIONS	SUGGESTED MODIFICATIONS

Adaptability

■ *The term "adaptability" is being incorporated into state and federal accessibility guidelines. Adaptable dwelling units are attractive and usable by anyone and are designed to be easily modified to accommodate people with physical disabilities.*

Are sinks, counters, and grab bars installed so they can be readjusted to different heights for different people?	Consider adjustable brackets on kitchen and bathroom counters and sinks as well as a continuous plywood backing in the walls surrounding a tub or toilet in remodeled bathrooms.

■ *The new ADA building specifications, designed to ensure accessibility of public buildings and multi-family housing, have generated new and similar ideas for achieving accessibility in private homes.*

Have you incorporated these specifications and ideas in your remodeling plans?	Consider, for example, a continuous corridor that is 3 feet wide, 6 feet 8 inches high, and free of hazards and abrupt changes in level to connect all important areas of the home. If such a pathway leads from the point where you enter to all important rooms, anyone, regardless of physical limitations, will be able to move easily around the home. Consider accessible appliances such as front-control stoves and side-by-side refrigerators.

References

Friedan, Betty. *The Fountain of Age.* New York: Simon & Schuster, 1993, p. 350.

Suggested Readings

Mace, Ronald L. *The Accessible Housing Design File.* New York: Van Nostrand Reinhold, 1991.

Please, Peter. *Able to Garden: A Practical Guide for Disabled and Elderly Gardeners.* London: B.T. Batsford Ltd, 1990.

Raschko, Bettyann Boetticher. *Housing Interiors for the Disabled & Elderly.* New York: Van Nostrand Reinhold, 1991.

Wasch, William K., and Anita Cox. *A Primer on Adaptable Housing for People with Disabilities.* Hartford, Conn.: Connecticut Task Force on Building Accessibility for State of Connecticut Office of Protection and Advocacy for Persons with Disabilities, 1991.

Wylde, Margaret, Adrian Baron-Robbins, and Sam Clark. *Building for a Lifetime.* Newtown, Conn.: The Taunton Press, 1994.

Chapter Five

Building a New Home

Getting Started

Building a new home can be the ultimate expression of your commitment to growing older comfortably and independently. If you have made the decision to build, you can take advantage of many of the new architectural concepts and age-friendly products introduced in this book. It is a significant challenge to move from the decision-making stage to the site selection, choice of architect, builder and other professionals, and development of a plan that meets your needs. Important considerations are:

- Do you want to build in a caregiver apartment?

- Do you want to build a single-family home or join forces with friends and build your own small community with some shared services?

Although it is important to work with an architect to ensure individualized plans, some of the "ready-made" plans for accessible housing can be useful. Examples include:

- The Adaptable Home, a highly affordable, fully accessible home designed by a partnership between the Lake County Housing Authority and Design for Independent Living, Inc., a Chicago firm specializing in accessible housing for seniors and people with disabilities

- The accessible one-story home designed by Lewis Homes in Orange County, California (a videotape of this design is available, which might be helpful to you during this research phase)

- The Middletown House illustrated in this chapter and available in a slide presentation

See the Appendix for details on each of these examples. Also included in the Appendix is information about specialized products discussed in this chapter.

Key Design Characteristics

A quick review of structural factors can help in achieving the combined goals of aesthetics and accessibility. Specific guidelines are recommended below.

Site and Location

- Face most windows south and east for maximum passive solar benefit. Windows should be on the south and east side of the home and heavy insulation should be on the north and northwest side.

- Consider views from the south and east side, and determine if trees will obstruct the view from windows.

Adaptable Layout

- Main living area should be approximately 2,200 square feet for owners on ground level with direct access from garage.

- Lower level or second floor caregiver apartment should be approximately 750 square feet for an individual or a couple.

Keep in mind this can at first be rented to tenants for extra income and later serve as a place for a caregiver to live.

- Garage should be on the ground floor with a separate entrance to the lower level or second floor to ensure privacy and maximum service for residents on both levels.

- Easy access to a lower or basement level for moving and delivery of any heavy items to basement utility space or lower level apartment should be provided.

Flexibility

- Design should permit changes in room use to eventually allow for complete wheelchair accessibility.

- The home should be accessible for a person with any limitation—vision, hearing, mobility, bathing, and so forth. A good standard to follow is found in the Activities of Daily Living (ADL) checklist. This standard should be applied to all parts of the house, especially any upper floors.

Security and Control

- Consider adding a home automation system which enables the total environment to be controlled from one spot and from a wheelchair, if necessary. Such a system allows the user to open and close windows, turn lights on and off, communicate with lifeline systems, and provides direct contact with fire, police, and other emergency services.

Special Kitchen and Bathroom Features

- The kitchen should have a completely accessible design compatible for individuals with any type of limitations. Include all modern conveniences, such as a microwave and adjustable counter heights, side-by-side refrigerator/freezer, and a seat at the sink, if necessary.

- The bathroom should have no-skid features, the latest type of equipment for bathing, showering, and toileting, and features that allow a person to sit at the sink and be showered and bathed, if necessary. A whirlpool bath and roll-in shower without a lip are other nice features. The bath should also be adaptable for a retrofit of the tub to accommodate a wheelchair-bound individual. Walls should be strengthened to accept grab bars if necessary.

- A dressing area should be included between the bathroom and bedroom for complete ease of dressing.

- A second bathroom should be added in the main part of the house for the caregiver and for use as a washroom or guest bathroom.

Maintenance

- Automatic snow melting system (e.g., heating coils in driveway) should be installed for houses in colder climates.

- A built-in central vacuum cleaner system should be included.

- Carpeting and rugs should be slip resistant and require little maintenance.

- The home's exterior should be easily repainted or stained, or low-maintenance siding may be considered.

- Landscaping should emphasize minimal lawn and garden care. Consider automatic sprinkling system and raised-bed gardens.

- Windows should be easy to open and clean. Consider the motor-driven window opening and closing devices.

Special Features

- Glare-free lighting throughout the house

- Balcony and/or larger deck off bedroom

- Screened-in porch off living room

- Fireplace or wood-burning stove

- Home video and stereo wall and/or "living room of the future" with wall-sized television set connected to computer system with access to worldwide information networks

- Home office in second bedroom wired and designed for latest computer and modem operation

The Middletown House

Although not yet constructed, the Middletown House is the result of a major research project based on an extensive collaboration among myself and three other professionals. They include Paul John Grayson, an architect/gerontologist who has conducted research in Europe and Japan, John Martin, a practicing architect and professor of architecture, and Christina Wasch, a recent graduate from the School of Architecture at the Massachusetts Institute of Technology (MIT), who worked with us on much of the design and product research. (Addresses and telephone numbers are in the Appendix.)

The Middletown House.

The Middletown House consists of a 2,200-square-foot accessible ground floor apartment and attached garage, with a 750-square-foot lower-level independent caregiver apartment. Until needed in this capacity, the apartment can be used for visiting family and friends.

The inter-relationships between plan and product emphasize the importance of appropriate design decisions and selection to minimize limitations imposed by disabilities, promote safety, and support daily living. In addition, the design should be responsive to the site and address aesthetic and psychological needs.

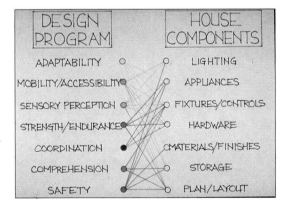

Effective site utilization maximizes the natural landscape and provides privacy.

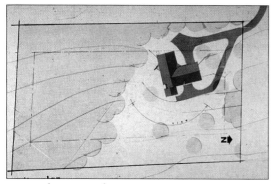

Site utilization plan.

The site for the Middletown House features a long, curving driveway.

The building site slopes downward from west to east, toward a pond on the left. The slope facilitated development of a two-level design with the main living area above a lower-level apartment. This allows those in both living areas to take advantage of the view toward the pond and yields a southern exposure. The driveway splits for vehicular access to both levels. The roof is composed of two intersecting gables.

The first floor can be reached from both the garage and the front door. From the garage one may enter directly, without steps, into the kitchen or foyer. The foyer can be adapted for access either to the house as a whole, or to privatize access to the two individual apartments.

The lower-level plan includes a utility room, basement storage, and an adaptable one-bedroom apartment. Many of the design features of the first floor are repeated in the lower-level apartment. In addition, special attention has been given to controlling airborne and impact sound between the two floors and mechanical systems.

Rubber tile flooring with a low-relief raised-disk pattern was selected for the first-floor foyer, staircase, and garage to help pre-

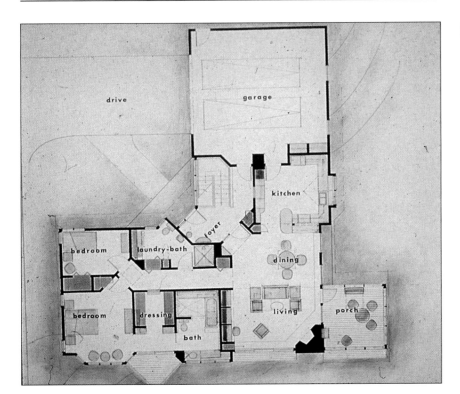

First-floor plan.

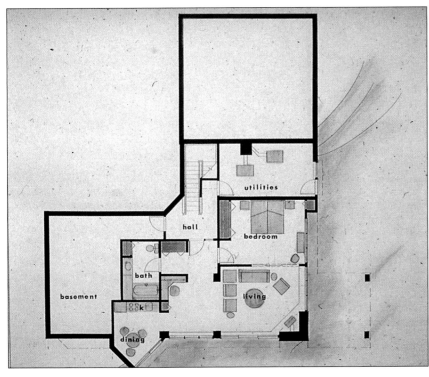

Lower-level plan.

vent falls. Stair colors have been chosen to clearly contrast rise and tread, although first floor residents will have little need to use the stairs.

Secure handrails are mounted on both sides of the staircase. These should contrast in color with the walls. As an adaptable feature, additional railings and grab bars could be installed in halls and bathrooms. Corridors are 4 feet wide and reinforced with blocking to support these future installations. Movement through the individual apartments is barrier free. This requires at least 3-foot wide doorways, with about 18 inches of clear space on the handle side of the door for pulling toward oneself.

- All hardware is operable with a closed fist.

- All swing, pocket, and bi-fold doors are fitted with a lever or large D-ring handles.

- Exterior door handles and keyholes are illuminated.

Skylights allow natural light into the room.

- Keyholders can help compensate for loss of fine motor coordination and strength. An escutcheon is a retrofit that would help glide a key into its proper position.

- Retrofitted handles, designed for those with motor handicaps, are especially helpful for crank-type operations.

Generous natural light during the day is provided by the home's southern exposure. To achieve solar gain while modifying high contrast, auxiliary lighting, primarily in the form of skylights, is introduced.

Skylights and other hard-to-reach windows are operated with a small electric motor. The motor features an exterior rain sensor that automatically closes the window when dampened. If the resident develops manipulation or mobility limitations in the future, all windows could be activated by such a motor.

A central vacuum system is built in for ease of cleaning and maintenance, as well as for its lighter weight and high-powered but quiet operation. Vacuum outlets are installed at least 18 inches above the floor. Higher baseboards and simple moldings also reduce bending and facilitate dusting.

An automation system controls the home's electrical systems. It can be programmed for individual needs and responds to both voice commands and touch control from anywhere in the house. For example, this device can open or close windows; turn lights and appliances on and off at programmed times or whenever desired; dial and answer the phone; communicate with a lifeline system, if necessary; and control heating and cooling systems.

Other types of home-service technology are also available and a complete list can be obtained from the Electronic Industries Association at P. O. Box 19100, Washington, DC 20036.

Roscoe the Robot is "employed" at the Danbury Hospital in Danbury, Connecticut. His general function is to perform time-consuming fetch-and-carry tasks throughout the hospital, such as delivering meal trays from the kitchen to the nursing stations. Another model similar to Roscoe is being developed for more specific home service applications. The "Homebot" will contain storage compartments for food and personal items, a telephone that travels to you, and a control panel that interfaces with the home's electronic systems. In the near future, this friendly and sophisticated robot will be able to, among other things, prepare and serve meals, clean the house, wash the car, take care of the grounds, act as a security guard, and even fix household appliances.

A storage/entertainment wall is located in the living room. Built-in storage systems are not only easier to clean but also make maximum use of space. A pull-out desk could be designed to fit into this wall system.

At the other end of the living room is a fireplace, and to its side is a sliding door leading to the screened porch. Depending on the climate, the porch could be adapted as a solarium in the winter or enclosed.

Kitchen

In the kitchen, which is reached through the dining room, the cathedral ceiling continues, following the gable line to the ridge. The kitchen includes a window over the counter, which provides a direct view of the driveway.

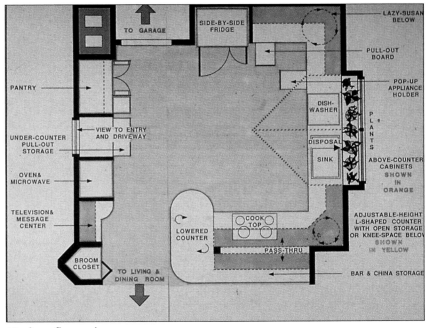

Kitchen floor plan.

This refrigerator/freezer is more easily accessed from a sitting position because of the exterior water and ice dispenser and side-by-side design. *Courtesy Whirlpool Home Appliance, Benton Harbor, Michigan*

- A skylight can be placed over the sink area, providing light to the back side of the kitchen as well as a pleasant view.

- A side-by-side refrigerator/freezer has been chosen for its accessibility. Other features of this appliance include adjustable shelving, self-defrost system, and an exterior water and ice dispenser.

- A pop-up appliance holder keeps the counters clear and small appliances easily accessible. Pull-out cutting board may also be equipped to grip a bowl or foods, leaving both hands free for mixing, slicing, and so forth.

The sink and stovetop are dropped into an "L"-shaped counter, which is open below and adjustable in height from 25 to 36 inches. This provides room for roll-out carts, kitchen stools, or wheelchair access. Cabinets above the counter also move up and down at the push of a button.

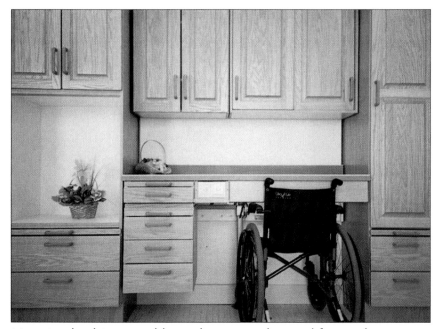

Motorized cabinets enable workspaces to be used from either a
sitting or standing position.
Courtesy of Superior Millwork LTD., Saskatoon, SK, Canada

Electrical outlets and controls are easily accessible at the front of the counter.

A lower-cost solution employs adjustable brackets for both counters and cabinets, similar to those used in some bookshelf systems. In each case, the sink would have a flexible drain pipe to accommodate the counter's changing height.

The faucet handle is an easy-to-operate lever, and its pull-out hose facilitates rinsing. The hose could also be used to fill pots on the cooktop.

Staggered burners with front-mounted controls are featured. Induction burners, which heat only the pot and not the stove surface, would be an additional safety option, although they require special cookware. Such a model is particularly beneficial for a visually impaired person. The

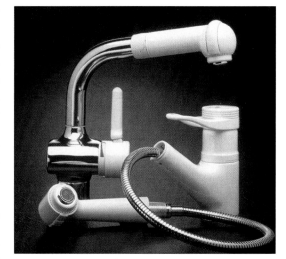

Fixtures such as faucet controls should be usable with a closed fist.
Courtesy Grohe America, Inc., Bloomingdale Illinois

controls light up when the burners are turned on and vary from yellow to dark orange, according to heat intensity. The lowered counter next to the cooktop is fixed at 30 inches; it provides an

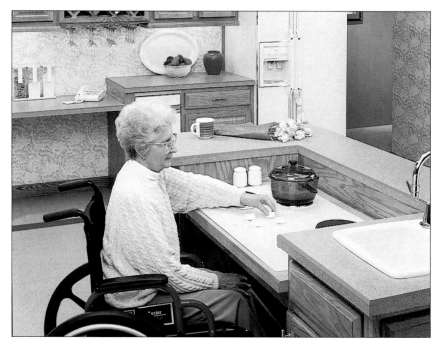

Accessible cooktops are available for use from a wheelchair.

Courtesy Whirlpool Home Appliance, Benton Harbor, Michigan

Under-the-counter placement of microwave oven permits easy access by all users.

Courtesy Whirlpool Home Appliance, Benton Harbor, Michigan

eat-in dining area as well as space for food preparation from a sitting position.

A microwave oven is mounted below the counter. If seated access is necessary, the wall oven should also have side hinges. Although the refrigerator design shown on page 136 is appropriate, its location should be modified to have counter space on both sides.

Pantry storage has adjustable shallow shelving. Its entire contents are visible at a glance. Access to pots, pans, and other cooking items stored at the back of cabinets is made easier with this arrangement. Large storage capacity provided by this unit will reduce frequent shopping trips.

A kitchen flooring that is grease and slip resistant, even when wet, is recommended.

If a kitchenette is planned for a lower-level apartment, it should incorporate design features such as under-counter slide-out storage, low-hung open shelving above, vertically mounted D-Ring hardware, a range with staggered burners and front controls, and an adjustable-height sink with an open knee space, if required.

Laundry/Bath

The laundry/bath area is intended as a combination guest bath and laundry. Upon entering, to the right is a fiberglass roll-in shower, measuring 4 feet by 4 feet.

The lavatory has a spring-loaded handle below the basin which easily adjusts the height of the sink from 19 to 36 inches.

A slide-out ironing board is chosen over the traditional stand-up types, or pull-down wall models, which are often heavy and hard to reach.

The washer and dryer, both front-loading, are installed 12 inches above the floor to reduce the distance one has to bend. This design also allows for a 3-foot-high folding counter with storage and hanging space above. On the left of the washer and dryer is a walk-through closet with storage space for both clean and dirty laundry. Beyond the laundry is a second bedroom, which could also serve as a study or exercise room. It is located next to the master bedroom in the event that a caregiver may someday need to be close by.

Front-loading washer and dryer for easy access from a wheelchair.

Courtesy Miele Appliances Inc., Somerset, New Jersey

Master Bedroom Suite

In the master bedroom suite, one closet is designed for medical supplies and any special equipment that might be needed. The bedroom is large enough for two single beds and a small sitting area. A sheltered deck, facing south and overlooking the pond, would be a pleasant place to sit.

- Ceiling joists are reinforced between bed and bath so that a lift can be installed, easing the task of transferring a bedridden person to the bathroom.

- To the right of the bedroom is an open dressing area. Clothing storage is made easy to access by using adjustable-height drawers, shelving, and hanging rods. Slide-out wire baskets show immediately where things are placed, without having to open drawers.

- For those with limited range of motion or in a wheelchair, a pull-down closet rod could be installed later.

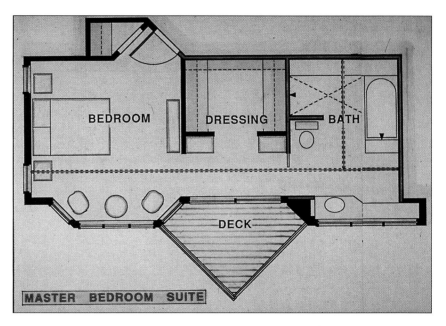

Master bedroom suite plan.

MASTER BEDROOM SUITE

- Past the dressing area is the master bath, a large skylit room, in which safety and accessibility, particularly for the person with the least mobility, were important design considerations.

- A pocket door makes it easier to move in and out of the room and is easier to open and close if mobility is limited.

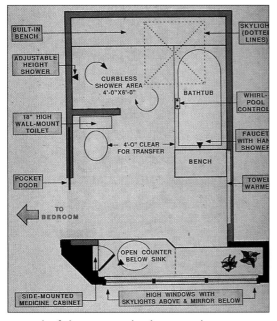

Detail of the master bathroom plan.

The tub and shower area is covered with mineral-impregnated anti-skid flooring, in effect helping to create a shower room rather than a stall. Mipolam is a type of polyvinyl chloride (PVC) sheeting. It is easy to clean; corners can be heat welded for water resistance; and compared with tile or other materials, it is not slippery when wet. A built-in bench can be covered with the same material, providing a warm, smooth, and secure surface to sit on while showering, being bathed, or transferring to the bath.

Accessible whether standing or seated, the adjustable shower fixture glides up and down, pivots 180 degrees, and may also be hand-held. The thermostat pre-sets the water temperature, preventing burns and assuring a constant temperature for the duration of the shower.

The fiberglass whirlpool bathtub has a textured bottom. The whirlpool controls are accessible during bathing, and the faucet includes a lever-style tap with hand-held shower which can also be used for cleaning the tub. A thermometer lets you know if the bath water is too hot or cold before you step into the tub.

The faucet is mounted to the side of the sink for easier access. The sink's drain pipe is flexible with the counter resting on adjustable brackets and open below, so that you can sit or stand while grooming.

Reinforced walls can be fitted with any type of towel rack or grab bar. There is also a mirror which tilts down for easier viewing when seated.

Perhaps the most innovative fixture in the bathroom is the Swiss-designed Closomat toilet, a combination toilet/bidet. The wall-hung model can be mounted 2 inches higher than standard for ease in sitting down, getting up, or transferring from a wheelchair. It is also easier to clean underneath the toilet.

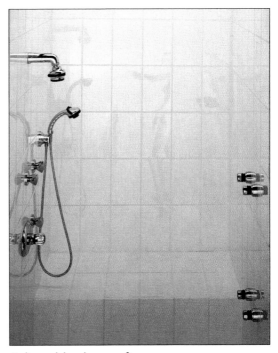

Adjustable shower fixture.
Courtesy Grohe America, Inc., Bloomindale, Illinois

The Middletown House is designed to work for everyone. Its solutions can provide for the fittest as well as the less able; such solutions attempt to support abilities rather than handicap them and to enable the individual rather than set up barriers.

The products discussed above can help you function independently longer, and also address aesthetic goals without calling attention to disabilities, thereby quietly supporting aging in place.

Although this house is designed for those with a higher income, the principles can be adapted to other designs.

Temperature-controlled bath and shower fixture. *Courtesy Grohe America, Inc., Bloomindale,*

Preparing for the 21st Century

Although the Middletown example includes many state-of-the-art concepts such as the home robot, it does not address environmental approaches to mental and intellectual stimulation that can be so important. Some of the most promising work is being done at the Livingroom of Tomorrow project at the Laboratory for Computer Science and the Media Laboratory. "Ours is a cozy living room because most of tomorrow's bits and chips will be consumed in the home. It is the natural venue in which to explore many future applications, like shopping, entertainment, and education. Reinventing the living room is not only natural but essential if our living spaces are to withstand the deluge of information and still be livable (Personal Information Architecture Group Brochure, 1994). The room is being designed and built in conjunction with Dean William Mitchell and the MIT School of Architecture." We already have the large screen TV sets on which a golfer can play the 18th hole at St. Andrews. Imagine the stimulation of doing this in an interactive way in the Living Room of the Future.

Another MIT project is the Body Net, which is an intimate infrastructure, that is, a personal network of wireless computers and appliances. This architecture envelops individual users and mediates between them and a world of external information systems including wristwatches, digital diaries, handheld computers, health monitors, pagers, and cellular communicators. This system will also relate to the Library Channel project, which will access the Library of Congress, National Geographic, and the Boston television station, WGBH.

Another very exciting new project in my home state of Connecticut is the information superhighway planned by SNET (Southern New England Telephone Company). This exciting technology will provide all homes with video-on-demand, other entertainment services, and access to vast databases; let students and schools exchange information via TV; allow hospitals, laboratories, and patients to relay test results and other information to each other; enable more people to work at home instead of in offices; and let motorists renew licenses without leaving home. SNET estimates the cost of this telecommunication hookup at $4.5 billion. The goal is to provide all homes and businesses with a one-step source for telecommunications, information, and entertainment services. SNET expects to connect 500,000 customers by 1997 and estimates that another 800,000 customers will be on-line by 2009. Fiber optic cables will link SNET's central offices to neighborhood equipment boxes, which will then be connected to customers' homes and businesses.

Every day hundreds of new computer users are entering the world of E-mail and electronic information systems like America

Online, Compuserve, Prodigy, and Senior Net. Although the Middletown House has some of these features such as a home automation system, the technology is developing rapidly, and a knowledgeable home automation professional should be consulted to advise you and your architect.

References

Personal Information Architecture Group Brochure, 1994, The Laboratory for Computer Science and the Media Laboratory, MIT 545 Technology Square, Cambridge, MA 02139.

Suggested Readings

Grayson, Paul John. Universal Design Products Serve All Regardless of Age. *Aging Network News* (McLean, Va.), April 1989.

Liebrock, S., and S. Behar. *Beautiful Barrier Free: A Visual Guide to Accessibility.* New York: Van Nostrand Reinhold, 1993.

National Association of Home Builders Research Center. *The Directory of Accessible Building Products.* 2nd Ed. Upper Marlboro, Md.: The Research Center, 1992.

Wasch, William K. A Dream House for All Ages: A New Niche for the Custom Builder. *Single Family Forum* 2(1):1 1990.

Chapter Six

Choosing a Retirement Community

Probably the most aggressively marketed senior housing options are the adult retirement/leisure communities and the service-oriented retirement communities. Just open your local newspaper and you will often see full page ads for programs similar to the one described as follows:

> For those who appreciate a valuable approach to retirement living. Beautiful surroundings and first class service, unlimited access to our professionally staffed, on-site Health Center, plus the Return of Capital Plan refunds up to 90 percent of your entry fee. All of these benefits are part of our life-care concept. Entrance fees begin at $150,000.

Confusing? Sure! Scary? You bet!

Because the issue is not simply a place to live, retirement communities represent one of the most complicated housing options. And the continuing care retirement community (CCRC) is the most difficult to evaluate because you will be making a sizeable investment in a home that you will not own in the same manner that one owns a house or a condominium. Moreover, initial costs, monthly costs, and ancillary costs are structured in different ways by each facility, making comparisons among different options especially difficult. Finally, you cannot anticipate future health and long-term needs, which makes it impossible to calculate total potential costs and returns on your investment. Nor can you easily measure or compare psychological benefits and "quality of life."

As a consultant, I have worked with many people to help clarify individual variables and establish objective criteria for comparing several facilities or communities that seemingly meet individual needs and preferences equally. A detailed example drawn from these consulting experiences is presented in this chapter to illustrate some of these criteria and to encourage a comprehensive evaluation before making any decisions or investing any money.

Leisure Communities

Leisure communities cater more to younger retirees and do not provide the extensive medical support programs traditionally found in most of the service-oriented retirement communities.

Significant differences between leisure communities and service-oriented retirement communities emphasize the importance of careful evaluation of your needs and a community's resources and retirement program.

Sun City, Arizona, is probably the best-known example of a leisure community in the United States. Originally built for healthy, middle- and upper-income individuals who wanted an active, yet leisurely lifestyle, these communities are generally low-density developments of permanent buildings offering "moderate to high" cost housing, for "active adults" over 55 years of age. They are equipped to provide a wide range of services with an emphasis on leisure activities. Residents are moderately affluent, physically able to take care of themselves, and are usually married (Heintz, 1976).

Rossmoor Walnut Creek, California, developed in the 1960s, represents another type of leisure community. A case study completed by Dale Romberg (1983) showed the difference between the developer's goal—an active retirement community—and the reality that existed in the 1980s. Its residents were 20 years older and in need of well-coordinated community and healthcare support.

These examples illustrate the importance of doing a thorough assessment, based on factors discussed in more detail in previous chapters. A few general guidelines that should be followed when considering a leisure community as a housing option include:

1. Complete the personal and community evaluations described in Chapters 1 and 2. Keep in mind the likelihood that your needs will change, and learn what each community can offer you now and later when you may have different abilities and limitations. For example, you may want a community right now that is close to shopping, but later you may have a need for Meals on Wheels or a congregate dining facility. As a result, each additional service becomes more costly and difficult to obtain.

2. Carefully evaluate current and future financial resources, as outlined in Chapter 3. Remember that many of the people who moved into leisure communities during the early years of these developments are now in their late 70s. Often they stretched their finances to purchase the less expensive cooperative townhouses. Because the community also charged a maintenance fee for additional services, and these costs have increased with inflation, the longer-term residents are now experiencing financial difficulties. For example, consider the impact of a 5% annual increase in maintenance over a 10- to 15-year period.

3. Carefully evaluate the accessibility of the units themselves. The guidelines identified in Chapters 1, 2, 4, and 5 can help in your analysis.

4. Finally, consider whether you want to live in an age-segregated community. As noted earlier, a way to overcome this limitation is to locate a community in a college setting. For example, at Eckerd College outside of St. Petersburg, Florida, housing for seniors has been constructed next to the campus. This results in considerable interaction between students and these older residents (including an academic program in which seniors are team teaching some of the courses). Similar communities have been established at Duke University and the University of North Carolina in Chapel Hill. A most appealing factor in these communities is the outstanding geriatric health programs such as the one offered by the Duke Medical School, as well as the availability of many cultural programs and classroom opportunities for seniors living there.

Service-Oriented Retirement Communities

These communities are the most difficult to evaluate because they range from rental communities that usually provide a daily sit-down meal, housekeeping, and transportation services to a continuing care retirement community (CCRC) that provides a full range of services from basic housekeeping and meals to full-time medical care. Both types of communities are designed to make life easier for residents. Because of their high costs, however, service-oriented communities primarily benefit middle- to upper-income retirees, and their costs vary depending on the type of facility, location, and the number of services available or used by the resident.

In general, service-oriented communities can be divided into three types:

- Rental retirement communities

- Assisted-living facilities

- CCRCs, or lifecare communities

Although these are general distinctions, sometimes you will find that terminology is used interchangeably, and it is important to note specifically what individual facilities have to offer. In particular, assisted-living facilities are usually part of a CCRC and represent a transition stage between an independent living cottage or apartment and an intermediate or skilled nursing home.

Case Example

Two older sisters, both widowed , participated in a very thorough consultation before making their decision about where to live. Both women were in their early 80s and lived on large adjoining properties in comfortable houses that they had bought and developed with their husbands during their retirement years. But now the struggle to obtain proper maintenance assistance and the distance from public transportation and medical services were making it more difficult for them to live there, so they had made a $10,000 down payment on a CCRC they thought would meet their needs. They called us for help, however, when they learned that this community was experiencing financial difficulty and that their initial investment might be at risk.

The first step in the consultation process was to develop an individual profile to determine precisely what type of retirement community would best meet their needs. The following profile was developed for them.

A specific, written list of needs and preferences will help you narrow the list of communities that warrant further consideration.

A Needs Profile

Based on discussions with the two sisters, their general criteria for a retirement community were as follows:

1. Location in central Connecticut, within 30 to 40 minutes by car from Middletown and/or Haddam. In addition, the community should be located so that one of the sisters could drive comfortably to New York City (probably no more than a 2- to 2 1/2-hour drive each way).

2. Ability to keep their two dogs.

3. Easy access to support services in the community so that one sister could stay in her New York City apartment for periods

of up to a week and be assured that her sister in Connecticut, who was in frail health, would be cared for in an unobtrusive way. It was important that the community could provide staff for a "security check" every few hours and also a personal emergency response system that could be activated by a help button either located on a chain around the neck or on a belt like a pager.

4. Long-term nursing facility on site. If either sister required assisted living or skilled nursing care, the other could easily visit. Furthermore, it was important that the community offered homecare services in case either sister required such assistance.

5. A wide range of amenities including quality food service, interesting social programs, and compatible residents.

6. Economic viability was an especially important criterion in view of their experience with another retirement community for which they had made a down payment but which was beginning to experience severe financial difficulty. Gathering this information would require research on the finances of the community, track record of owners and managers, long-term care insurance to guarantee long-term healthcare reserves, and age distribution of residents.

The first priority, therefore, was to research the first community and determine whether it was still financially viable and what steps, if any, could be taken immediately to protect these women's investment. This experience underlines the flaws in many state systems even when the state office certifying CCRCs has legislation to protect the finances of CCRC residents and to assure the future financial viability of these often-complex organizations.

Our first step was to interview knowledgeable individuals from the area, check their responses against each other to be sure they were consistent, and then make a final determination. On the basis of these reports, we recommended not pursuing the original community further at this time. The likelihood of a successful operation in the face of a large number of openings at other viable CCRCs and rental retirement communities around the state was very slim, and the risk of losing their entry fee was too great to justify proceeding with the women's original plan.

Other Options: Four Rental Retirement Communities and Six CCRCs

Due to the geographic limitations imposed by the two sisters, facilities were selected on the basis of a maximum distance from their current homes. To provide a full range of communities, including those only providing meals, housekeeping, and bus transportation as well as those offering a full continuum of care, we selected the following communities.

Rental Retirement Community #1

The first rental retirement community (RRC) evaluated was a three-story apartment building with 131 living units clustered around a common area with a dining room, auditorium, library, bank, and post office. The overall complex also included 73 cottage apartments, 57 single room accommodations, 60 single assisted-living rooms, a 90-unit intermediate and skilled nursing facility, and an adult day care center serving up to 60 participants. Located on 120 acres, this RRC is 100 miles from Boston and 100 miles from New York City.

An active social program sponsored by a social director and the tenants' association, one meal per day, free transportation to shopping areas and medical appointments, full security, cleaning, assisted-living, and monitoring services are all available. Pets are allowed.

The apartments and garages are rental units. All other facilities on the site from the independent living cottages to the skilled nursing facility are available on a daily or monthly fee basis.

A large two-bedroom unit with a den (1,120 square feet) is available for $2,941 per month. A garage can be rented for an additional $37 per month.

Rental Retirement Community #2

This community consists of a three-story apartment building with 52 living units. On the ground floor of the facility there is a dining room, health spa, library, card room, beauty salon/barber shop, and country store. Located on 7 acres, this RRC is 100 miles from Boston and 110 miles from New York City.

Socialization is always important, and dining facilites and meal plans should be included in your evaluation.

An active social and activity program organized by a social director, free transportation to shopping areas and medical appointments, full security, cleaning, and monitoring services are all available. Daily meal service in the dining room is optional. Pets are allowed.

Weekly nurse consultations and 24-hour on-call nursing services are provided.

The apartments are for sale, and a monthly fee for services is charged. Any homecare services required can be arranged with the local visiting nurse association or other homecare service. A large two-bedroom apartment (906 square feet) on the ground floor can be purchased for $116,000. The monthly fee is $689 with an additional $330 per month for one daily meal for two people.

Rental Retirement Community #3

This community consists of a three-story apartment building with 174 living units. On the ground floor there is a dining room, lounges, library, auditorium, beauty/barber shop, and activity room. Among the 174 units are 14 apartments adapted for an assisted-living program. Located on a 20-acre site surrounded by a lake, this facility is 120 miles from Boston and 90 miles from New York City.

An active social and activity program coordinated by a social director and tenants' association, daily meal, free transportation to shopping areas and medical appointments, full security, cleaning, and monitoring services are all available. Pets are allowed.

Private nursing, home health, and companion services are available on a fee-for-service basis. More extensive medical and homecare services are offered through a special assisted-living program administered on a fee-for-service basis.

The apartments are direct monthly rentals and include the standard services. The assisted-living program is in addition to the standard monthly rental and is contracted for on a monthly basis.

A large, two-bedroom unit (1,095 square feet) rents for $2,700 per month.

Rental Retirement Community #4

This community consists of a three-story apartment building containing 78 living units with a common dining room, library, and activity center. The complex also includes 44 separate cottages and a separate small apartment building with 12 units. A 160-bed intermediate and skilled nursing facility is currently under construction on the site. Located on 450 acres, the complex is 120 miles from Boston and 80 miles from New York City.

An active social and activity program organized by a social director and a tenants' association, daily meal, free transportation to shopping areas and medical appointments, full security, cleaning, and monitoring services are all available. The complex includes walking trails, a fitness center, tennis courts, and an outdoor swimming pool. Pets are allowed.

Private nursing, home health, and companion services are available on a fee-for-service basis. The entry fee was refundable up to 90%. The apartments are direct monthly rentals, which also cover standard services. A large, two-bedroom apartment (893 square feet) has an entry fee of $148,400 and rents for a monthly fee of $2,173.

Continuing Care Retirement Community #1

This complex consists of 114 apartments and a 116-bed intermediate and skilled nursing facility. The apartments are on three levels and are connected by closed hallways that lead to central common areas such as the dining room, library, club room, and several other facilities. The 116-bed nursing home is a separate building across the parking lot from the retirement apartment building. Located on 15 landscaped acres, it is 80 miles from Boston and 120 miles from New York City.

Types of regular and special-occasion activities can be compared among different communities you are visiting.

An active social program coordinated by an activities director and the tenants' association, one meal per day, free transportation to shopping areas and medical appointments, full security, and cleaning are all provided. Home healthcare as needed is available at no extra cost in the apartments. Pets are allowed. An all-inclusive contract is offered with 90% refund policy. A monthly fee is additional.

A large, two-bedroom apartment (1,000 square feet) for two has an entry fee of $140,000, and a monthly service charge of $2,395 for two. A portion of the monthly fee covers long-term care insurance. Also included in this monthly fee, because these individuals would be entering at age 83 and 86, is an additional senior service fee of $97 per month and $198 per month, respectively. If one person is in the health center and the other remains in the apartment, there is no change in the monthly fee.

Continuing Care Retirement Community #2

This CCRC comprises 76 independent living cottages and 98 apartments in two- and three-story buildings clustered around a common area with a dining room, auditorium, library, bank, and post office. Located on a 168-acre site surrounded by woods and a pond, the community is 120 miles from Boston and 90 miles from New York City. The community adjoins a 200-acre site where there is an 86-bed facility for the aged and a first-class 482-bed intermediate and skilled nursing and medical care facility and clinic.

An active social program coordinated by an activities director and the tenants' association, one meal per day, free transportation to shopping areas and medical appointments, full security, and cleaning are all provided. Assisted-living services are available in the cottages and apartments through the local visiting nurses association and homecare organizations on a fee-for-service basis. Pets are allowed.

A modified contract is offered with full entry fee refund during the first year. The refund is reduced an equal amount each year until no refund is available after 8 years. A monthly fee is additional.

A large, two-bedroom apartment (967 square feet) has an entry fee of $171,900, and a monthly service charge of $1,819 for two. This monthly fee includes the premium on a long-term care insurance policy for each of the two residents. This policy provides up to $40 per day of homecare or $80 per day nursing facility care for up to a total of 2 years. Additional homecare and nursing facility fees over and above this monthly fee must be paid.

Continuing Care Retirement Community #3

This facility includes three distinct three-story apartment buildings with 216 living units clustered around a village green and connected to a common area with dining room, auditorium, library, bank, post office, greenhouse, and a 60-bed medical care facility and clinic. Located on 72 acres of woodlands and meadows, it is 100 miles from Boston and 120 miles from New York City.

An active social program coordinated by an activities director and the tenants' association, one meal per day, free transportation to shopping areas and medical appointments, full security, cleaning, and assisted-living services are all available.

Assistance with errands and other off-site activities may be important in maintaining independence.

An all-inclusive contract is offered with full entry fee refund up to three months after moving in and an 80% refund less an additional 2% for each additional month. (In effect, there is no refund of the entry fee after 50 months of residence.) The monthly fee is additional.

A large, two-bedroom unit (1,126 square feet) for two has an entry fee of $137,000 and a monthly service charge of $3,854 for two. The monthly fee is the same in the nursing facility as in the apartment. If one person is in the health center and the other remains in the apartment, there is no change in the monthly fee.

Continuing Care Retirement Community #4

This facility contains four types of independent living apartments serving 42 residents, a congregate living facility with 60 units of private and semi-private spaces, and a 90-bed skilled nursing facility. Located on 33 acres, the community is 80 miles from New York City and 120 miles from Boston.

A nondenominational organization, this CCRC discourages the use of alcohol and tobacco. Services include one midday meal for the independent living units and all meals in the congregate section and nursing facilities. The independent living units provide routine maintenance, bimonthly cleaning, utilities, and an emergency call system as well as a preventive care program. Homecare is available for apartment residents on a fee-for-service basis. An active social program coordinated by an activities director with a tenants' association is in place. Other common facilities include a library, woodworking shop, and conference room. Pets are allowed, with management approval. Skilled and intermediate nursing care are not included in the independent living package. They are provided on a fee-for-service basis.

This complex cannot be classified as a full continuing care retirement community because the monthly fee for the independent living apartments does not include healthcare in the intermediate and skilled nursing facility. These are available on a per diem basis. If two people such as these sisters lived in the independent living unit and one needed to go to the skilled nursing facility, one would pay the single fee for the apartment and the other would have to pay the per diem nursing home fee. This could become very costly.

An entry fee with a 50% refund is required for the independent living units. The monthly fee is additional. The congregate private and semi-private rooms have no entry fee but a substantially higher monthly fee. Nursing care for residents in these rooms is on a per diem basis. For example, the per diem private room rate for the skilled nursing facility is $236 per day.

The entry fee for the largest independent living unit (980 square feet) is $202,000 with 50% refundable to the residents or their estates. It has a monthly fee of $1,531 for two.

Continuing Care Retirement Community #5

This facility comprises several three-story apartment wings of 216 living units connected to a common area with dining room, auditorium, library, bank, post office, an indoor swimming pool, and a 35-bed medical care facility and clinic. Located on 104 acres of woodlands and meadows, it is 100 miles from Boston and 90 miles from New York City.

An active social program coordinated by a social director and tenants' association, one meal per day, free transportation to shopping areas and medical appointments, a nine-hole golf course, full security, and cleaning are all available. Assisted-living and monitoring services are provided in the apartment. Pets are allowed, but a $1,000 fee must be deposited as insurance against damage. An all-inclusive contract is offered with a 90% entry fee refund. The monthly fee is additional.

A large, two-bedroom apartment with den (1,206 square feet) has a current entry fee of $326,000, and a monthly rental fee of $2,410 for two. The monthly fee is the same in the nursing facility as in the apartment. If one person is in the health center and the other remains in the apartment, there is no change in the monthly fee except for the cost of the two extra daily meals.

Continuing Care Retirement Community #6

This community includes 37 cottages, 118 apartments, and a 109-room health center (consisting of 49 congregate units, 30 assisted-living units, and 30 intermediate and skilled nursing units). The apartments are on three levels and are connected by closed hallways to the common areas, which include a dining room, library, auditorium, classroom, and several other facilities.

The four healthcare sections extend out from the common area and surround a central courtyard. Located on 66 naturally landscaped acres, it is 100 miles from Boston and 120 miles from New York City.

An active social program sponsored by the activities director and the tenants' association, one meal per day, free trans-portation to shopping areas and medical

CCRCs can combine personalized living space with service-oriented common areas.

appointments, full security, cleaning, and home healthcare as needed are all included at no extra cost in the apartments and cottages. Pets are allowed. An all-inclusive contract is available with three types of refund policies. These range from a full 67% refund at any time following occupancy to a full refund less 2% for each month of residency. Each of the three plans, however, has a different total entry and monthly fee.

A large, two-bedroom apartment (920 square feet) with the full 67% refund plan has a current entry fee of $216,699, and a monthly rental charge of $2,370 for two. The monthly fee is the same in the congregate, assisted-living, and intermediate and skilled nursing facility as in the apartment. If one person is in the health center and the other remains in the apartment, there is no change in the monthly fee.

Community Attributes and Personal Guidelines

The next step in our consulting program was to evaluate all of the communities based on how they fit the specific needs of the two potential residents. After this was completed the sisters made personal visits to the top four communities on their list and spoke with residents in order to sense the ambiance of the facility and decide whether they felt they would get along with the other residents. Issues of privacy, social factors, and the supportive environment of the facility are often harder to assess and might require several visits to the facility at different times as well as a thorough reading of the material provided by management.

We have included two checklists on pages 159 to 162 that would allow careful evaluation of these four communities or any community you might want to consider: Real Costs Checklist and Facility Costs and Amenities Comparison Checklist. The reviews called for in these checklists often require the assistance of a professional consultant for a complete evaluation and review.

The following analysis reveals how the 10 communities we evaluated measured up to our clients' expectations and needs.

- All ten communities will meet the distance and pet guidelines.

- All ten communities can provide the "security check" and monitoring program either as part of the all-inclusive contract or on a fee-for-service basis.

- All ten communities can provide homecare services in the apartment either as part of the all-inclusive contract or on a fee-for-service basis. All but two have nearby intermediate and skilled nursing care facilities either as part of the all-inclusive contract, partially covered by long-term care insurance, or entirely on a fee-for-service basis.

- All ten communities offer a wide range of amenities and services. The food service, quality and availability of social programs, and compatibility question, however, will require personal visits and further research because of their importance to the quality of a resident's life.

- The financial stability and future of all ten communities are vital issues to be assessed, and this research is best begun only after the clients have narrowed their personal choices to three or four preferred communities. In addition, these will have to be further evaluated based on the clients' decisions regarding financial arrangements (i.e., all-inclusive, modified, or fee-for-service contracts) that best meet their needs and desires. (See Real Costs Checklist and Facility Costs and Amenities Comparison Checklist for details of these evaluations.)

Real Costs Checklist

1. Entry fee

2. Refund

3. Net entrance fee

4. Monthly fee

5. Lost opportunity cost:

   (Based on 6.0% Treasuries)

   (Fee: X .06% / 12 months)

6. Total real cost: Monthly

7. Long-term skilled nursing care insurance premium

8. Total cash cost: monthly

Facility Costs and Amenities Comparison Checklist

Costs for Entry and Monthly Fees

1. What is the entry fee?

2. What is the monthly fee?

3. Will any of the entry fee be refunded?

4. Are there any terms affecting the percentage of a refund, such as duration of residence?

5. What are the variations regarding the refund policy?

6. Which healthcare services, including personal care services provided in the apartment are covered in entry and monthly fees?

7. Are utility and cable television costs included in the monthly fee?

8. Are housekeeping, daily meal(s), activities, and scheduled transportation included in the monthly fees?

9. Is there a limit to increases in monthly fees?

10. What has been the history of monthly and entry fee increases? (Review a 5-year history or number of years since opening.)

Nature and Extent of Healthcare

1. Does the community provide a full range of healthcare aide service and support for activities of daily living in the apartments? Are costs covered by the regular healthcare program?

2. Does the community have and provide a continuum of care such as access to congregate and assisted-living units before the intermediate and skilled nursing facility?

3. Is access to these healthcare facilities as well as to the intermediate and skilled nursing facility guaranteed?

4. How many beds are in the congregate care and assisted-living facility, if any?

5. How many beds are in the intermediate and skilled nursing facility?

6. Presently, how full are these facilities?

7. Is a registered nurse on-call 24 hours a day?

The Apartments

1. Is a large, two-bedroom, two-bath unit on the ground floor presently available?

2. If not, can two adjoining units be combined to make such a space?

3. If so, what would be the revised entry and monthly fee over and above a standard two-bedroom and two-bath unit?

4. Are pets allowed?

5. Is immediate occupancy available or is there a waiting list?

6. If there is a waiting list for a large unit that will best meet your needs, what kind of timetable is projected?

7. Are the apartments, especially the kitchen and bathroom, designed to accommodate changing needs? For example, are the bathroom and shower accessible to someone using a walker or wheelchair? Can grab bars be installed where they may be needed?

8. How quiet is the apartment? Is it well insulated for low sound transmission between units and hallway?

9. Is there adequate storage space available to residents in addition to adequate apartment closet space?

10. Are residents satisfied with maintenance support?

Food Service Management and Dining

1. Are residents satisfied with the quality and service of the dining room?

2. Is there flexibility in the dining facilities to permit choice of meal times and locations? For example, is there a snack bar and does the food service staff arrange special events during the year to keep dining more enjoyable?

3. How many different entreés are offered each day?

4. Does the dining room offer special menus to accommodate personal dietary needs?

Security and General Quality of Life

1. Is the community attuned to daily well being and safety without being intrusive?

2. Does the facility have a centralized electronic system monitoring smoke detectors, emergency response, heating, lighting, and other mechanical systems?

3. Will the community provide transportation to and from medical appointments?

4. What type of social programs, excursions, and cultural activities are offered?

5. Can the community increase its number of units and alter the present environment? What is the long-range expansion plan, if any?

Management and Financial Viability

1. Has the management surveyed residents to measure their satisfaction with all aspects of life in the community? If so, what were results?

2. What is the experience and background of the management, board of trustees for nonprofit facilities, and owners?

3. What is the age distribution of the present residents?

4. How does the community propose to pay for future healthcare costs?

5. How much of the per resident *monthly* fee is set aside for future healthcare?

6. How much of the per resident *entry* fee is set aside for future healthcare?

7. How much will the general financial reserves be, on a per resident basis, when the community is fully occupied?

8. How many years of experience in adult healthcare does the management have? What is the financial viability of the community? Can the management provide a copy of the disclosure statement as well as annual financial reports and projections?

Recommended Plan of Action

Our first recommendation was to initiate action to secure the release of their $10,000 entry fee deposit for the previously targeted facility. In view of the above, it was advisable that both women immediately begin to make personal visits to those communities most likely to best meet their guidelines. Community and facility preferences were divided into three groups in order of preference:

First Choices: The "All-Inclusive" or Full-Service Communities

These communities were ranked number one by the clients for the following reasons:

- All four have a reasonable combination of entry fees, refund policies, and monthly fees for the all-inclusive contracts that they offer. They all provide total lifecare in the same location and permit in-apartment support as well as a "security check" program when residents are away.

- All are located in central Connecticut and within a 2- to 2 1/2-hour drive from New York City.

- All have a reputation for excellent services, and it is likely that both clients would be compatible with the residents. These more subjective characteristics, however, will be better judged by personal visits and follow-up contacts with current residents.

- More research will be required to assess the financial viability of each of the four chosen communities. Further analysis of the resident agreements and disclosure statements will be necessary in order to make these determinations. The age distribution, how full each of these communities presently is, and a comparison of past and projected increases in monthly fees should also be reviewed. For example, from additional research, it was discovered that one community was increasing fees considerably above the customary annual increase of 2% to 5%.

- A problem at another facility was a long waiting list, but one that can move quite fast depending upon the type of unit desired. The two-bedroom units are the slowest to turn over, which could be a concern for these clients.

Second Choices

The reasons for these choices are as follows:

- One is operated by an organization that has an excellent reputation. While the monthly rental fee is high, there is no entry fee. This is substantially offset, however, by the fact that all higher levels of care are on a fee-for-service basis including in-apartment homecare. A personal visit is a must as well as research on the facility's financial situation. This community also offers a unique adult day care center, which can be of considerable assistance to residents with dementia.

- One rental community with a high entry fee was a second choice because it provides in-apartment homecare on a fee-for-service basis and will have an on-site nursing home on the grounds in 2 years, available on a per diem basis. It has a low monthly fee but a high entry fee, which is, however, 90% refundable.

Third Choices

Four facilities were placed in the third category. The reasons were as follows:

- Two facilities only refund half of their high entry fees but have very low monthly fees. Of the two, one has the better long-term care arrangement because its monthly fees cover some long-term care and homecare through a long-term care policy. At the other, this must be paid for entirely on a fee-for-service per diem basis.

- Two others have similar rental rates as well as some assisted-living apartments, which offer in-apartment assisted-living services on a fee-for-service basis. These facilities, however, have no on-site nursing facility, which can create a very difficult situation if one of the two residents requires nursing facility accommodation.

Summary of Findings

The next steps included an open and frank discussion of the report and plan of action with the two clients, immediately followed by appointments and personal visits to the first-choice communities. It was very helpful to use the checklists presented on pages 159 to 162 to record observations and help make more detailed comparisons. Then, together with their advisor, they rated the four and decided whether any of the second- and third-choice communities should be visited. Once the final group was identified the financial research was completed to help make a final decision.

These facilities met most of our clients' guidelines, and all are more age-friendly for the older resident. Staged living in which a variety of services and housing arrangements permit a resident to remain in the same community regardless of needs, is certainly one of the main features of the CCRCs. This is not the case in the rental retirement communities except for those places that have an in-apartment homecare program. Transportation is supplied in all instances, and all of the facilities take pride in their amenities, which include high-quality dining room service and extensive social, cultural, and recreational opportunities.

It is important to determine how accessible the common areas are in these facilities. For instance, those facilities built more recently are much more accessible from the parking lot to the apartment. Another had high straight back chairs in all the common areas to make it much easier for their elderly residents to stand up and sit down. But even the newest ones do not have state-of-the-art bathroom and kitchen accessibility. Often the bathrooms rely on the institutional-looking stainless steel grab bars that are, at times, improperly installed. A more sophisticated accessibility assessment would be helpful for potential residents as well as the management, which still has a difficult marketing job to sell the service-oriented retirement community concept to the senior market. The key design characteristics described in Chapter 5 can be helpful in evaluating accessibility for older and frailer residents.

Conclusions

As it is so provocatively stated by Betty Friedan in *The Fountain of Age* (1993):

> Strangely enough, though my mother spent the last twenty five years of her life in a "retirement" community for "active" older people, devoted to play, walled off from the fears and danger and problems of our changing larger society—walled off from change altogether, including the changed attitude toward themselves and other reminders of their own aging in the communities they left behind—that very denial of age and change left her helpless in its inexorable progression, torn from any semblance of home and personal, rooted bonds.

Newer retirement communities today are built around nursing homes, even if the facility is walled off from the rest of the community or hidden in a remote wing or top floor. I visited many of these "congregate care," or "continuing care," or "lifetime care" communities, thinking they were surely the answer to denial, avoiding the trauma of my mother's forced move and decline before death. But, as I visited the best of them—near Philadelphia; in Charlotte, North Carolina, as well as in Florida and California—I began to wonder if there aren't worse things than denial. With increasing uneasiness, I began to wonder if the people I interviewed who had bought into these facilities to save their children from "having to put me in a nursing home" weren't defining themselves, too soon, as objects of such ultimate "care." Were they, in fact, somehow *colluding* in the process of denying their own personhood by withdrawing into that "care" ghetto? They were defining their age, not in terms of purposes and choices and ties to life, but in *defense against death*, in terms of terminal care (p. 374).

With this type of thinking moving us closer to "quality of life" issues we may very well see a major movement in the United States toward less age-segregated housing and farther away from the medical model in old age. Certainly hospice, the living will, and other national movements to avoid high-level medical intervention suggest that these ideas as well as the European models are beginning to inform our own thinking in the United States.

We will certainly see efforts to separate housing and services. The current long-term care policy in the United States is primarily to package housing and personal care through Medicaid by paying for both only in a licensed nursing facility. The more progressive community-based approach would separate housing and service reimbursement so that housing and services could be paid separately, thereby providing older persons with a broad set of choices of where to live. Thus they would not have to move to a nursing facility to obtain the care they need. With more choices some would choose group-living situations, such as assisted-living or supportive housing, and others would try to stay in their own homes as long as possible. But the first step will be for federal policy to allow Medicaid waivers for some home-care and home modifications and combine them with housing vouchers—a direction beginning to be set in the United States by the European experiences and the forward-looking program in the state of Oregon.

Because we all want to remain independent for as long as we can, the most desirable scenario is to stay in our own private home or apartment as long as possible. As we discussed in Chapters 4 and 5, we can either build a new accessible home or modify our home or apartment to meet accessibility guidelines and possibly delay future moves to more dependent living facilities for a longer period of time.

If we choose some of the options discussed in this chapter, however, we still should review the questions discussed in Chapters 2 and 3 before making such an important life decision. Questions like "elder friendly," up-front, entry, and continuing costs such as those required by CCRCs, other options ranging from mobile home parks to ECHO housing, availability of on-site or nearby medical clinics, access to staged living based on changing needs, transportation, and accessibility are issues of great importance in making these decisions.

In conclusion I cannot emphasize enough the importance of conducting the type of review outlined in this final chapter on service-oriented retirement communities. It is crucial to understanding this complicated form of senior housing. This is even more important when we see how aggressively these facilities are promoted to a group of seniors who often want to avoid a move to these lifecare communities unless all other options fail. On the other hand, they have much to offer. Should a family develop a range of medical problems, the insurance offered by such a community can be of inestimable value to both the seniors and their children. So we encourage you to do your personal forecasts, research your options, evaluate your resources, and develop your plan for that later year "house in the high wood within a Walk of the Sea" as eloquently described by Hilaire Belloc.

References

Friedan, Betty. *The Fountain of Age*. New York: Simon & Schuster, 1993.

Romberg, Dale. *A Study of Rossmoor Leisure World*. Master's Thesis. California State University, Hayward, California, 1983.

Heintz, KM. *Retirement Communities for Adults Only*. New Brunswick, N.J.: Rutgers University Center, Center for Urban Policy Research, 1976.

Suggested Readings

Callahan, James J. (ed.). "Aging in Place" Generations. *Quarterly Journal of The American Society on Aging* Spring:1992.

Chapman, Elwood N. *Life Care: The Inside Story*. Menlo Park, Calif.: Crisp Publications, 1994.

Hare, Patrick H., and Jolene N. Ostler. *Creating an Accessory Apartment*. New York: McGraw-Hill Book Company, 1988.

Pastalan, Leon A., and Benjamin Schwarz (eds.). University-linked Retirement Communities: Student Visions of Eldercare. *Journal of Housing for the Elderly* November: 1994.

A Few Last Words

Now that I reflect on my research, the many individuals and organizations with whom I have worked to develop these ideas, and their complicated and interrelated nature, I am more than ever convinced of the critical need for more long-range planning and careful evaluation of what we can do to make our home environment more responsive to the physical and mental changes which take place as we age. So I have established a new direction for my consulting firm to work with individuals and small organizations to begin this planning process with individuals in their 50s. There is no reason why each of us should not have a plan in place to deal with these important issues in a way which will emphasize quality-of-life questions. I also hope to continue my education and advocacy efforts. I will work with national aging organizations to ensure that all professionals in both the housing and aging fields are aware of these ideas and can help many more of the aging baby boomers come to grips with these issues in designing their own homes for their later years.

For further information on the book and these consulting plans, please contact me at William K. Wasch Associates, 150 Coleman Road, Middletown, CT 06457, 860/347-2967 or fax 860/347-8459.

William K. Wasch
Middletown, Connecticut
December 1995

Appendix 1: Product Information

The following resource list includes many of the products referred to or discussed in Chapter 4, Modifying Your Present House, and Chapter 5, Building a New Home.

Allstate Rubber Corporation
105-12 101st. Ave.
Ozone Park, NY 11416
718/526-7890
(Tractionfloer, slip-resistant vinyl sheets)

Anderson Windows, Inc.
100 Fourth Avenue, North
Bayport, MN 55003
612/439-5150
(window motor cranks and pull-locks)

Aquarius Industries
Route 1, Box 46D
Savannah, TN 38372
800/223-8827
(roll-in showers)

BPS Architectural Product
10816 Fallstone Road
Suite 505
Houston, TX 77099
800/255-9513
(barrier-free architectural products)

Clairson International/Closet Maid
650 S.W. 27th Avenue
P. O. Box 4400
Ocala, FL 34478
800/227-8319
(closet and cabinet storage)

Cervitor Kitchens Incorporated
10775 Lower Azusa Road
El Monte, CA 91731-1351
818/443-0184
800/523-2666
(compact kitchen units)

Dwyer Products Corporation
418 North Calumet Avenue
Michigan City, IN 46360
219/874-5236
800/348-8508
(accessible kitchenettes)

Electrolux Corporation
800/243-9078
(central vacuum systems)

G.E. Appliances
Appliance Park
Louisville, KY 40225
502/452-4311
(cooktops, microwaves, and ovens)

Grohe America
241 Covington Drive
Bloomingdale, IL 60108
708/582-7711
(kitchen, lavatory, and shower faucets)

Hafele America Company
P. O. Box 4000
Archdale, NC 27263
910/889-2322
800/334-1873
(pull-down closet rods, storage systems and hardware)

HEWI, Inc.
2851 Old Tree Drive
Lancaster, PA 17603
717/293-1313
in Canada — 800/293-6359
(bathroom accessibility products)

HomeCare Suites, Inc.
805 East Maple Road, #310
Birmingham, MI 48009-6449
810/644-5757
(mobile accessory apartments)

Ironmonger
122 West Illinois Street
Chicago, IL 60610
312/527-4800
(illuminated levers and keyholes)

Johnsonite
16910 Munn Road
Chagrin Falls, OH 44023
216/543-8916
800/637-4995
(rubber stair treads)

Life-Light
810 Monroe Avenue
Asbury Park, NJ 07712
908/775-2522
800/545-4470
(smoke detectors for hearing impaired)

Lindustries, Inc.
21 Shady Hill Road
Weston, MA 02193-1407
617/237-8177
(doorknob lever adapters)

Mastervoice
10523 Humboldt St.
Los Alamitos, CA 90720
213/594-6581
(home automation systems)

Miele Appliances Inc.
22D Worlds Fair Drive
Somerset, NJ 08873
908/560-0899
(washers, dryers, and cooktops with illuminated controls)

Roppe
1602 North Union Street
Fostoria, OH 44830
419/435-5645
800/537-9527
(raised rubber disk stair treads and nosings)

Schulte Corporation
11450 Grooms Road
Cincinnati, OH 45242
513/489-9300
800/669-3225
(adjustable storage systems)

Superior Millwork LTD.
2502 Thayer Avenue
Saskatoon, Saskatchewan
CANADA S7N 2T1
306/374-9440
(motorized, adjustable cabinets and countertops)

Valli & Colombo, Inc.
P. O. Box 245
Duarte, CA 91009
818/359-2569
800/423-7161
(retro handles and key holders)

Villeroy & Boch, USA, Inc.
Interstate 80 at New Maple Avenue
Pinebrook, NJ 07068
800/558-8453
(adjustable lift sinks)

Whirlpool Home Appliances
800/253-1301
(accessible kitchen and laundry)

There are many other products that would be of interest to individuals modifying an older home or building a new one, and we refer our readers to three other books, *Beautiful Barrier Free: A Visual Guide to Accessibility, Building for a Lifetime,* and the NAHB Research Center's *Directory of Accessible Building Products,* listed in the Suggested Readings. All three have excellent product information lists and will be a helpful supplement to the above list.

Appendix 2: Housing and Community Services Information

American Association of Retired Persons
AARP Fulfillment
601 E Street, NW
Washington, DC 20049
(Write for their extensive list of publications on various aging issues.)

Coastal Colony Corporation
2935 Meadow View Road
Manheim, PA 17545
(General information on Echo Housing.)

Design for Independent Living
7549 North Oakler
Chicago, IL 60645
312/973-4776
(General information on adaptable homes.)

Elderhostel
100 Boylston St., Suite 200
Boston, MA 02116
Registration 617/426-8056
Administration 617/426-7788
(Write for catalogue of vast range of education programs for seniors in the United States and other parts of the world.)

Manufactured Housing Institute
1745 Jefferson Davis Highway, Suite 511
Arlington, VA 22202
703/413-6620
(General information on manufactured and mobile homes.)

National Association of Home Builders and Remodelers
1201 15th Street, N.W.
Washington, DC 20005
202/822-0200
(Write for their extensive list of publications on new housing, remodeling, and product research by the NAHB research office.)

National Council on Aging, Inc. (NCOA)
409 3rd Street, S.W.
Washington, DC 20024
202/479-1200
(Makes available a major library on aging issues including a broad range of books and booklets. Provides a very helpful publication entitled *Senior Center Standards and Self-Assessment Workbook,* 1990 to use to evaluate community resources.)

National Eldercare Institute on Housing and Support Services
Andrus Gerontology Center
University of Southern California
University Park, MC-0191
Los Angeles, CA 90089
(Write for their extensive list of publications on housing and supportive services.)

National Shared Housing Resource Center
321 East 25th St.
Baltimore, MD 21218
410/235-4454
(Provides a variety of booklets and other information on shared housing.)

Recreational Vehicle Industry Association
800/336-0154

Shepherd's Centers of America
6700 Troost, Suite 616
Kansas City, MO 64131
(Write for information on their 90 Centers around the country, all of which are operated by seniors for seniors. Their work will illustrate what retirees can do to build and strengthen voluntary programs for seniors.)

As in the case of products, there are several books that provide invaluable background information on reviewing and evaluating senior services in a community. We refer our readers to two other books, *Housing Options and Services for Older Adults* and *Social Services for the Elderly,* listed in the Suggested Readings. They will be a helpful supplement to the above list.

Appendix 3: Consultants

Paul John Grayson, AIA
Environments for Living
P.O. Box 698
Winchester, MA 01890
617/721-1920

John Martin, AIA
129 Little City Rd.
Higganum, CT 06441
860/345-4900

Christina E. Wasch, Architect
45 Cottage St.
Cambridge, MA 02139
617/661-8091

Video and Slide Resources

A Home for All Ages Video
Mary H. Yearns, Ph.D.
Iowa State University Extension
62 LeBaron Hall
Ames, Iowa 50011
515/294-8520
(A video demonstrating a range of assistive devices and design features in a fully accessible house.)

The Hartford House Video
The Hartford Insurance Group
Hartford Plaza
Hartford, CT 06115
860/547-3488
(A video featuring a wide range of home adaptations.)

The Friendly Home Video
Consumer Affairs Office
Southern California Gas Co.
Box 3249
Los Angeles, CA 90051
213/244-4354
(A video featuring adaptable features of a new home in Chino, CA.)

Adapt Your Home Video
William K. Wasch Associates
150 Coleman Road
Middletown, CT 06457
860/346-2967
(A video displaying a range of home accessibility problems and a set of low-cost solutions usable in private homes and large housing complexes.)

The Middletown House Slide Show
William K. Wasch Associates
150 Coleman Road
Middletown, CT 06457
860/346-2967
(A two-tray slide show with accompanying narrative highlighting the design and products used in planning this fully accessible one-story home with lower-level caregiver apartment.)

Index